THREE
OF THE
FIRST

THREE

OF THE

FIRST

HILTON OWENS, SR.

iUniverse, Inc.
Bloomington

Three of the First

iUniverse books may be ordered through booksellers or by contacting:

iUniverse
1663 Liberty Drive
Bloomington, IN 47403
www.iuniverse.com
1-800-Authors (1-800-288-4677)

ISBN: 978-1-4502-3363-7 (sc)
ISBN: 978-1-4502-3364-4 (hc)
ISBN: 978-1-4502-3365-1 (ebk)

Library of Congress Control Number: 2011909639

Printed in the United States of America

iUniverse rev. date: 11/03/2011

Contents

Author's Note

This is not a work of fiction, although the chronology of events were sometimes altered to lessen the likelihood of innocent persons being identified or embarrassed. Any resemblance between the characters in this book and real persons is not coincidental.

We were among the first African-American special agents to serve a full twenty years in the Internal Revenue Service, Intelligence Division (now Criminal Investigation), and retire.

This is not a spine-tingling novel of intrigue depicting the exploits of three heroes. We were not heroes. It is the story of three ordinary guys, who happened to be African-American, and should be remembered as part of Black history, and also as part of the IRS family.

Our careers, as well as our lives were similar, but yet so different. We marched to different drummers.

A Special Note

A considerable portion of this book relates to the Undercover Agents. This is because I, as well as many other African-American special agents (criminal investigators), figured prominently in the undercover activities over the years. My partner gave his life.

I have imposed on Dan Bonomi, retired Supervisory Criminal Investigator, to discuss this specialized training and work, inasmuch as he eventually headed this elite centralized group, which operated out of the National Office in Washington, D.C. His remarks are contained in another section of this book.

Dedications

To—   My family and especially Supervisory Special Agent
        Jerome C. Owens, who decided on his own, to follow me.

To—   The late Special Agent Curtis D. Patterson, my partner and
        friend who gave his all.

To—   All my special agent friends throughout the Service and
        retired.

A Special Thanks to

Danny
Still my best friend and confident who also paid some heavy dues.

Albert
My brother. He knows why.

Bea
For all the reasons.

Acknowledgements

Special thanks to the people at the IRS National Office who furnished me valuable statistical data and other information that went a long way in making this book a reality. Assistant Commissioner Bruce V. Milburn; and my longtime friend Branch Chief Sandy A. Stephens and her staff. Also, special thanks to another friend Patricia C. Francis and her staff, of the EEO program, for their most enlightening material.

A special thanks to Assistant Professor Vicki S. Vorell, CPA, who tolerated me in her recent federal taxation classroom. More important, she gave new life to my manuscript that was about to start gathering dust.

Preface

The first income tax law was created by the Revenue Act of 1913, and imposed a one percent tax on income of individuals, estates, trusts and corporations. A surtax of one to six percent was imposed on income exceeding $20,000. Rates, exemptions, and deductions have changed many times since the tax law was first imposed.

The divisions of the Internal Revenue Service that are most familiar to the taxpaying public are the Collection Division, whose Revenue Officers collect delinquent taxes, and the Examination Division (formerly known as the Audit Division), whose Internal Revenue Agents examine tax returns and books and records to determine the tax liability.

There is, however, a relatively little-known division, called the Criminal Investigation Division (formerly the Intelligence Division), whose Special Agents investigate tax fraud.

As early as 1919, then Commissioner of Internal Revenue Daniel C. Roper had repeatedly received allegations of widespread tax fraud, also serious corruption in the Bureau of Internal Revenue.

Prior to becoming head of the Bureau, Commissioner Roper had served as an Assistant Postmaster General and was familiar with the Postal Inspector's work, which involved investigations of mail fraud and dishonest postal employees. Commissioner Roper was successful in obtaining approval from the Secretary of the Treasury and the Postmaster General to transfer six postal inspectors to the Bureau of Internal Revenue. On July 1, 1919, these six inspectors became the first special agents in the Special Intelligence Unit, under the leadership of 31-year-old Elmer L. Irey. He held the position of Chief of the unit from July 1, 1919 until January 1943. However, starting in 1937, he also held the position of chief coordinator for all Treasury law enforcement agencies.

Others who joined Irey in 1919 were Hugh McQuillen, Frank Frayser, Herbert E. Lucas, Arthur Nicols, Everett Partridge and Arthur Smith.

The unit expanded to 21 by mid-1920; 112 by 1925; and 200 by 1935. During their initial years the men of the Special Intelligence Unit had three primary responsibilities; investigate suspected dishonesty of Internal Revenue employees; investigate submission of fraudulent tax returns and other attempts to evade taxes; and investigate charged of unethical conduct by persons admitted to practice before the Treasury Department.

The Special Intelligence Unit continued to grow until 1951, when it was split into the Intelligence Division, which was concerned primarily with tax fraud investigations, and the Inspection Service, which dealt with internal security matters.

The Intelligence Division underwent a final name change in 1978 when it was designated the Criminal Investigation Division. Irey served as the unit's chief until January 1943, when he devoted all his time to coordinating all Treasury Department enforcement activities. He retired from government service in 1946.

During Irey's many years with the unit, the special agents became known as the "giant killers." It was not Eliot Ness and the Untouchables who brought about the downfall of Alphonse "Al" Capone, but an income tax evasion conviction in1931, which resulted in 10 years in a federal penitentiary and one year in the Cook County jail.

Another interesting case, in which income tax was not involved, was the Lindbergh baby kidnapping. Colonel Lindbergh asked that the Secretary of the Treasury have the Special Intelligence Unit join the Attorney General of New Jersey in the investigation. The recording of the serial numbers of the ransom money (gold certificates) by special agents of the special intelligence unit played a major role in the apprehension of Bruno Richard Hauptmann. When Hauptmann was arrested, part of the ransom money was found. Later at the trial, a special agent's testimony proved that the Hauptmanns' net worth and expenditures approximated the amount of the ransom paid. Hauptmann was convicted.

Over the years the Special Intelligence Unit continued to build on its impressive record of convictions. A person's station in life, occupation, or political or financial status has never deterred the division in seeking out and recommending prosecution of alleged tax evaders. Bureau employees were no exceptions.

The first case investigated by the unit involved two certified public accountants and an Internal Revenue Inspector. It was a highly publicized case that served notice to taxpayers and Bureau employees alike that a specialized unit had been organized to investigate and recommend prosecution for attempted bribery, extortion and other dishonest acts. Revenue officers, revenue agents, special agents, reviewers, and cashiers have been tried, convicted, and removed from the Bureau. A former IRS Commissioner, Joseph Nunan (1944-1947), was convicted of income tax evasion in1954, and sentenced to five years imprisonment and a $15,000 fine. Mathew Connelly, President Truman's appointments secretary, and T. Lamar Caudle, head of The Department of Justice Tax Division, were convicted in1957 of conspiring to defraud the United States in connection with a tax investigation. In 1973, Vice President Spiro Agnew resigned and pleaded "no contest" to evading income taxes. He received probation and a $10,000 fine. Rock star Charles E. Berry (aka Chuck Berry) pleaded guilty to tax evasion and was placed on probation on the condition that he perform 1,000 hours of community service, including concerts and charitable activities. The division did not neglect the truck driver who claimed five non-existent children; the schoolteacher who suddenly claimed several children as dependents—her pet cats had the same names as those listed on the tax return; the "madam" who failed to file; or the doctor or lawyer, who systematically failed to report fees received in cash from patients or clients.

In the late 1920s many Hollywood motion-picture stars were investigated for income tax improprieties. Many entered pleas of guilty to tax evasion, while other cases were settled civilly.

The organization has always maintained a low profile, but its history of successfully convicting would-be tax evaders speaks for itself. The following is a list of individuals who directed the unit since its inception in 1919:

Directors of the Intelligence Division
(Criminal Investigation Division)
1919-1986

Elmer L. Irey	1919-1943
W. Harry Woolk	1943-1951
Frank Lohn	1951-1952
Garland Williams	1953-1953
A. Walter Fleming	1953-1955
J. Perry August	1955-1959
H. Alan Long	1959-1965
William A. Kolar	1965-1970
Robert K. Lund	1970-1972

John J. Olszewski	1972-1975
Thomas J. Clancy	1975-1982
Richard C. Wassanaar	1982-1986

In 1989, at the time this book was compiled, the division was relatively small, having 2,723 special agents, including 531 females. The special agents are officially known as Criminal Investigators. They have statutory law enforcement powers, resulting in hazardous duty, and as a result are eligible for early retirement at age 50 with twenty years service in the Criminal Investigation Division. There are recent changes that permit special agents with 25 years in the division to retire at any age, and mandatory retirement was recently changed from age 55 to 57.

National Office officials advised that in 1989 there were 197 African-American special agents, including 67 females, in the Criminal Investigation Division. At that time, the agents on board held a variety of field, supervisory and managerial positions.

Retired Assistant Regional Commissioner of Criminal Investigation—Frederick L. Sleet, one of the subjects of this book, attained one of the highest positions among African-Americans. A female African-American now holds a similar position.

George N. Carlton, Jr. was appointed to the position of special agent in the Pittsburgh District in August 1953 and thus became the first African-American special agent in the nation. However, he did not serve a full twenty years in the division. His career will be discussed later.

This book relates to the Intelligence Division in general, and the careers of three African-Americans in particular. They were among the first to be appointed to special agent positions in the Service, serve a full 20 years, and retire. Their order of appearance in the book is based on their entry date into the division, as illustrated by the following:

Name	CID Entry Date	Retirement
Hilton Owens, Sr.	January 30, 1955	January 31, 1975
William E. Mannie	January 25, 1959	January 4, 1984
Frederick L. Sleet	January 7, 1962	January 3, 1983

What is a Special Agent?
They have been called the "silent investigators."

They have been called the "giant killers."

They have been called unmentionable names, but even then, with respect.

What is a Special Agents' Job?

Succinctly, to investigation alleged violations of the internal revenue laws.

Naturally, the federal system requires a more detailed and comprehensive job description of the criminal investigators' duties and responsibilities.

The textbook job description for special agents reaching the top field grade (GS-13) read in part, when we were in the service, as follows:

Classification: Criminal Investigator, GS-1811-13
Organizational Title: Special Agent

Duties and Responsibilities (excerpts)

"Plans and conducts tax evasion investigations potentially of wide scope, or extreme complexity, or major importance involve extremely controversial matters. highly delicate issue require the exercise of a high degree of ingenuity and resourcefulness obtain facts from obscure sources take appropriate action to protect the Government's interest."

Each of us worked within these guidelines as special agents until we advanced to Supervisory Criminal Investigator (group manager) and later to management positions. In the latter positions (beyond special agent) we retained our law enforcement/hazardous duty status, as we still participated in field activities.

For publicity and for advertising special agent vacancies in the division, a poster was prominently displayed at college recruiting seminars and similar gatherings that would attract would-be candidates.

Introduction

These are the stories of three ordinary people who decided that they wished to investigate tax evaders. Each of us has served in other divisions of the Internal Revenue Service and was not a stranger to the activities of the Intelligence Division. Little did we realize at the time that we would later be singled out as pioneers.

Being personally and professionally associated with the Other Criminal Investigators (special agents) included in this book, I am confident that a complete historical or fictional account of their lives and activities could fill volumes.

Further, certain activities in which we were involved may only receive vague or passing comments. That is deliberate, because of the sensitive nature of many of our assignments. This book is not intended to furnish detailed information regarding the division's investigative techniques, but rather a chronology of events and activities of each of us climbing the career ladder.

PART I

Hilton Owens, Sr.

The first African-American criminal investigator (special agent) to serve
twenty full years in the Intelligence Division and retire.

Chapter One

It was February 7, 1975 and John J. Olszewski, director, of the IRS Intelligence Division, was concluding a speech before a group of my friends and co-workers at Andrews Air Force Base Officers' Club in Washington, D.C., honoring me on my retirement after more than thirty-one years of federal government service, the last twenty of which were served in the Intelligence Division. He concluded his speech by reading a letter he had written to me that day, which touched me deeply.

It stated,

"Dear Hilton,

Thirty-one years of government service, on paper, appears to be a long time. However, you and I know how swiftly the time has passed. I am told this is the experience of life when one is challenged by his work, develops the skill as an expert and achieves the satisfaction of outstanding accomplishment and success which is recognized by his peers and associates.

Your expertise in all facets of financial fraud involving all forms of business activity—legal and illegal—will be sorely missed. However, we do have the satisfaction of knowing that you are leaving a successor and protégé, who may someday surpass all our achievements, your son Jerome. I know of no greater testimonial to the fine example you have set for all of us as well as your son.

As Director, I extend my sincere appreciation and gratitude on behalf of all your associates in the Service for your willing assistance, complete dedication, commitment and, most important, your friendship.

We all extend our sincere best wishes to you and Beatrice for an equally long, healthful, happy and successful retirement.

Most sincerely,
John J. Olszewski
Director, Intelligence Division"

Other speeches followed, but my mind and eyes drifted over to familiar faces in the crowd; particularly my wife by my side and my three children and family, most sitting facing me. The only thing I could think of was how had all those years passed so quickly. I recalled that my wife informed me after one of my long absences from home that one of the children asked, "What does daddy look like?" I was then ready to "come in from the cold," a term used when undercover operatives leave the field and take a desk job. I will never know how I managed to remain in the field as an undercover agent for so many years.

However, at the conclusion of the speeches, when asked to say a few words, I choked, and my faithful friend Group Manager Dick Cotner came to my rescue (again). It was an event that I will never forget. We special agents repeated many of our "war stories." My family had an opportunity to meet my co-workers and friends, and as will always happen, my sister, two brothers and I reminisced about our childhood days.

I was born on January 21, 1924 in Cleveland, Ohio. The world was at peace. President Coolidge was in the White House, Andrew Mellon was Secretary of the Treasury, and Herbert Hoover was Secretary of the Interior. Ohio State University was about to pass 10,000 enrollment. Men suits cost $22 and shirts cost $1.30. Henry Ford was offering his New Touring Car-Ford five-passenger open car for $295. A child's deluxe sled cost $3.95 and Maxwell House coffee was "good to the last drop." One could purchase a four-bedroom colonial house in Shaker Heights, a swank Cleveland suburb, for $15,000. Newspaper comics included Mutt and Jeff, Barney Google, and Penne Ante. Tris Speaker was manager of the Cleveland Indians. Al Jolson and John Barrymore would be coming to the downtown Hanna Theater soon. Cleveland had its first City Manager form of government, replacing an elected mayor. The city later reverted to the elected mayor system.

That was the world into which I was born, the second of eventually a family of four children, an ordinary child in an ordinary African-American family trying to survive. My father worked in a foundry at the time of my birth, and two years later joined The Standard Oil Company of Ohio (SOHIO) in the same capacity, where he remained until he retired on disability in the 1960s. My mother did "day work." They somehow managed to house, clothe and feed us. We were happy children. I am sure our parents worried a lot because of the chronic lack of money, but it never dawned on us that we were poor. After much discussion, and seemingly years of waiting, The Standard Oil Company paid its employees a bonus. We thought that our father was rich, and he gave each of us the staggering sum of 25 cents, which made us rich as well. We treated all of our neighborhood friends with their choices at the nearby candy store. Our older and wiser brother Fred placed a limit of one cent on each friend's purchase. Long after our 25 cents was spent we still controlled the neighborhood kids, who thought more money and candy would be forthcoming. Eventually things returned to normal.

As I look back on those years, there were no "pockets of blacks" or ghettos, and as a small child I recall Mrs. Little Bear (a full-blooded Indian) living on one side of us and our Italian friends living on the other. I recall living in other mixed neighborhoods of Polish and Hungarians. These were the Great Depression years. Our neighbors were in the same financial circumstances as ourselves and sometimes worse, because my father always worked for Standard Oil Company and had some small amount of pay every two weeks. Some of our neighbors were less fortunate but everyone survived. If there were racial tensions, we children were not aware of it.

As children, my sister Margaret and her friends played with dolls, while my brothers, Fred and Albert, and I were avid readers. Each of us read every book we could get our hands on at the libraries, from older children, and any other source. We became very knowledgeable about the stars in the universe and Buck Rogers of the 25th Century taught us all about space travel; while our religious parents considered such talk as blasphemous, they did not attempt to dissuade us in our quest for knowledge. The library history books taught us about the old west and the settling of the pioneers. We visited castles in Europe as we read of King Arthur and his Knights of the Round Table. Sir Lancelot was my favorite. We learned of physics and electricity from books that taught us how to build crystal sets and telephones. The crystal set's reception depended on weather conditions. The homemade telephones were connected to friends nearby. Our younger brother Albert, even before he was old enough for school, joined in assembling our "contraptions." As a matter of fact, Albert's intelligence far surpassed his age in that even before he started school he could read and write, and also beat everyone playing checkers, including my father's friends, who bragged of their checkerboard prowess. They usually left our house sadder and wiser. I would not be surprised if a few dollars passed hands between my father and his friends after these sessions.

We were definitely ahead of our time, which sometimes caused problems in school and church, but we generally kept our theories about science and religion to ourselves.

Overall, our childhood was full of rich achievements. We were FBI agent Melvin Pervis' junior G-Men, and faithful radio listeners of "Gang Busters." We prided ourselves in solving crimes before the one-hour radio programs ended.

Christmas meant a huge turkey dinner with all the trimmings. Our Christmas socks were always filled with hard candy, apples and oranges, and we always received some new clothing, and toys. As youngsters, we faithfully wrote letters to Santa Claus, c/o the *Cleveland News*, one of our local newspapers, asking for all types of toys that we had a premonition we would not receive in our Christmas stockings. Without fail and generally on Christmas Eve, a *Cleveland News* delivery truck would bring some type of toy for each of us. What more could a small child want? How could we Owenses ever look back and complain about our childhood? It was quite amusing how practical we children were insofar as Christmas was concerned. At a very early age we concluded that it was scientifically impossible for Santa Claus and his reindeer to travel across the sky without a source of energy similar to that used by Buck Rogers of the 25th Century. We accepted our parents' explanations of Santa Claus until they decided that we children had "given them the business" long enough.

My teen years were uneventful. I managed to stay out of jail, much to the surprise of my parents, and went to church (not voluntarily) all day every Sunday. I somehow managed to graduate from Central High School in Cleveland, Ohio in June 1942, with three letters in track and exceptionally good grades. It was from Miss Mary Alice Ryan's English class that I learned of Langston Hughes, W.E.B. Dubois, and Booker T. Washington. Miss Ryan, a Caucasian, saved many of us from total ignorance insofar as African-American history was concerned. There were no formal African-America history classes taught at our high school.

A year after high school, I was drafted into the Army where I served four years, two of which were in the European Theater of Operations. The military is where I received my first taste of racial prejudice. I recall leaving Camp Perry, Ohio by train, with former white schoolmates and arriving in Camp Lee, Virginia. Blacks and whites were sent in different directions. I did not see my white school friends again. We few "northerners" in our army units were constantly being criticized by our southern fellow-soldiers for being so ignorant of our African-American heritage.

While overseas, my childhood sweetheart and later-to-be wife enlisted in the Women's Army Corp (WACs), trying to follow me. Her outfit, minus the younger WACs, made it to England and France, and we were, at one time, bivouacked in the same general area. She was among the younger girls that were left behind. We were married in December 1945 in Cleveland, Ohio, while both on leave. She was discharged in March 1946. I completed my regular army tour of duty and was discharged in April 1947. I immediately obtained employment with the Veterans Administration as a clerk typist, earning $1,954 per year. I knew that the GI Bill paid for all books and tuition plus $120 per month to veterans attending college. As a husband and new father, I needed the education, but the money even more. I enrolled in the evening division at tiny Fenn College, (now Cleveland State University). The university now has a sprawling, thriving, campus in downtown Cleveland. After two years of evening classes at Fenn College, I transferred to then Western Reserve University (now Case Western Reserve University), and graduated with a Bachelor of Business Administration degree in September 1953. We had three children by that time. My daughter, then seven years of age, was permitted by her school to attend my graduation ceremonies at Severance Hall, if she agreed to relate the experience to her classmates. The setting for the graduation was the majestic home of the Cleveland Symphony Orchestra and was a building that present-day adults still find most impressive. Even today, that now middle-aged daughter remembers her daddy in cap and gown receiving his degree.

Chapter Two

Prior to completing my degree requirements I joined the then Bureau of Internal Revenue as a Zone Deputy Collector, now known as Revenue Officers. After graduating from college, I took another civil service examination for Internal Revenue Agent/Special Agent, which I passed and was accepted in the Audit Division as an Internal Revenue Agent. Up to that point my life had been uneventful. Whether I had worn blinders like a racehorse or had looked at the world through rose-colored glasses is not for me to say. I suppose my church upbringing would not have permitted me to feel that because of past racial discrimination and inequities in our society, the world "owed me"; the syndrome that presently prevails in much of the African-American community. So in all my endeavors I took the position that I did not need, or ask for assistance from anyone, and if I did not receive any interference when I tried to do my best, success was assured.

Thus, becoming one of the first African-Americans in the Collection Division, Audit Division, and the Intelligence Division in the Cleveland District just seemed to me to be something that happened in the normal course of events. I have always contended that the Cleveland District, even back in the early 1950s, was an equal opportunity employer, before it became fashionable or mandatory. That is not to say that there were not bigots scattered throughout the organization, just as in any large organization, but they were not in the majority and I could deal with them. I always remember my mother-in-law (and good friend) saying to me, "son, you've got to be ready when opportunity knocks." She was right, and I was ready. I recall another African-American no-nonsense guy, my good friend Fulton Barnett, who rose to a chief's position in the Cleveland IRS District, describe me as "ruthless—a true winner," which I considered a rather harsh statement at the time, but after thinking about it, if he meant that I would not tolerate interference or obstacles from my superiors, peers, or subordinates in achieving an objective, he was right. My lengthy government career sorely tested my theories, convictions, and beliefs.

Chapter Three

Audit Division Field Audit
Cleveland District 1954

It was late in 1954 in Cleveland, Ohio and I had returned to the office from an audit of a taxpayer's return. Our telephone receptionist advised me to call the acting chief, Myron B. McCammon, Intelligence Division. Returning his call had a profound effect on the rest of my career and personal life. He informed me that I had been selected to be interviewed the following day for a special agent position with the Cleveland District Intelligence Division, as a result of me having formally expressed an interest in becoming a special agent. As I look back on the interview, I feel it was an administrative formality, and that I had already been selected for the position if I decided to accept. The only question I recall being asked by one member of the panel (later to become my supervisor and good friend), was whether I was aware of the fact that I would be a pioneer in that there were no other Negro special agents in the Internal Revenue Service. At this writing I am having difficulty recalling my response, but apparently my answers to those questions relating to my ethnic background were satisfactory, because in late 1954 I was officially notified that I had been selected for a special agent position. This would be officially classified as a reassignment because special agents and internal revenue agents held similar grades and salaries and were normally selected from the same civil service register, which required at least a bachelor's degree, with a major in accounting.

On the same day, I also received a telephone call from Internal Revenue Agent Curtis D. Patterson, another African-American and an attorney, whom I knew only as a co-worker and speaking acquaintance. He advised me that he had been selected for a special agent position and had heard through the grapevine that I was also selected. Neither Patterson, who was to become my best friend, nor I had the slightest idea that our professional and personal lives and those of our families would forever intertwined.

Like me, Patterson had a wife and three small children. Later events brought our families close together.

Why did I transfer to the Intelligence Division? During the 1950s the Bureau of Internal Revenue lived up to its bureaucratic image. As a matter of fact, the agency's name change to the Internal Revenue Service was intended to help in changing the agency's image to a service-oriented organization. Internal Revenue Agents and Revenue Officers had well-defined monthly production quotas based on their grades. Agents in lower grades were required to complete the greatest number of cases each month, but such cases were the less complicated, while higher grade agents were required to produce fewer in number, but more complex in issues. I had no difficulty as a deputy collector (revenue officer) or an internal revenue agent in meeting, and exceeding my quotas, in dollars and numbers. These statistics were prominently posted on the unit's bulletin board each month. It was actually a competitive game to me, and I always made sure my name was at or near the top of production statistics each month. As a deputy collector I recall a humorous incident in which I "hit the jackpot" one month and submitted more cases than my entire group combined. I had so many telephone calls that month that our group receptionist jokingly "grounded me." That is, she suggested that I "cool it" until the rest of our group could catch up. My group supervisor remained silent, but our group was the standout in the division that particular month and many times thereafter.

This game became monotonous to me and after several years of collecting delinquent taxes, I transferred to the Audit Division. As an Internal Revenue Agent, I examined books and records of taxpayers to determine their correct tax liabilities. Pressure to complete specific numbers of cases was ever-present. I met and exceeded the quotas with ease, but I had difficulty in accepting the Service's policy regarding production quotas, which they preferred to categorize as "production goals," a less ominous term. I silently rebelled against the production quotas and the only way I showed my displeasure was to "overproduce" each month. That was my silent protest. While Service officials vehemently denied that promotions were based on these quotas, the agents on the firing-line knew better. One school of thought on the production concept was that agents might, and often did, become overzealous in their dealings with taxpayers, and opponents of the production quotas, such as the forerunner of the National Treasury Employees Union (NTEU), eventually prevailed.

Chapter Four

At the first opportunity, I requested and was accepted by the Intelligence Division as a special agent. Neither as an agent or a first-line supervisor did I concern myself with production quotas or goals. My primary concern for myself as an agent, or the performance of agents under my immediate supervision, was completion of successful criminal cases, whether it required six months or several years. In the Intelligence Division I had finally found a home.

Word rapidly circulated throughout the Service that the Cleveland District had two African-American special agents onboard. It seemed to Patterson and me that the entire country had been waiting, and wanted to "borrow" us for special assignments. Why did they not hire their own African-American special agents? Patterson and I knew the answer to our own question. The Cleveland District was an exception, but the Internal Revenue Service in general was not an equal opportunity employer.

The situation outside the Cleveland District caused us to wonder aloud whether trading our calculator and 13-column accounting pads for a new pocket commission, a gold badge and a .38 Smith & Wesson revolver had been a wise move. Time would tell. Patterson and I constantly joked to each other, "Treat me nice, because I'm the only friend you've got." That was true in the sense that special agents, particularly those involved in clandestine activities, seldom made new friends, and old friendships eroded as we frequently disappeared and reappeared without explanation.

We had been in the Intelligence Division only a few short weeks when we received our first undercover assignment. "Undercover, what's that?" we asked. We were soon to learn. Of all places to send two rookie special agents, we were sent to the south side of Chicago, which conjured up images of Al Capone and Eliot Ness, blues singer Jimmy Rushing belting out;

> "Going to Chicago,
> Sorry that I can't take you.
> There ain't nothing in Chicago
> That a monkey woman can do"

There we were, thrown into that underworld jungle, driving a personal car, with license plates registered to either Patterson or myself. We carried no fake ID, and even a fender bender accident could have compromised our identities. IRS did not furnish us funds for travel in those early years. We had to use our personal funds for meals, lodging, and incidentals such as money for gambling, or hanging out in clubs. Our early travel vouchers for reimbursement of monies spent caused uproars. Travel vouchers such as ours, claiming reimbursement for drinking and gambling were like hot potatoes that no one cared to approve. All the while, waiting for our expense checks to arrive, our travel vouchers were passed from hand to hand. On many occasions our lack of funds and survival in those ghettos depended upon how well we did at the gambling establishments we frequented, or whether we picked winners at the track. We were lucky at both.

We knew that there was no one to whom we could turn for advice. As time passed we were amused to learn that we were considered the 'experts' in this field. Our activities in Chicago are still most vivid in my mind's eye, but because none of our activities were made public in open court, it would be inappropriate to discuss the nature of this first most sensitive assignment. Suffice it to say that we worked out of the U.S. Attorney's office at the time.

For all intents and purposes, we received our baptism of fire and Chicago street education at the Squeeze-Inn Bar on Chicago's south side in early 1955. I recall a barmaid or customer asking Patterson what he did for a living, he replied, "as little as possible." When I was asked the same question, I responded, "I help him." The rest of that first afternoon was a hilarious elbow-bending marathon. New York had the reputation of being "the" swinging town, but Chicago also had it all: jazz music, cheap booze, wide-open gambling, lip-smacking barbeque ribs, chitterlings, and all those other foods, that are now referred to as "soul food." The Windy City had an almost southern hospitality. That friendliness and openness did not fool us for a minute. Violence and death were commonplace, because of arguments mostly over women, gambling debts, or someone just attempting to establish a reputation. Hard drugs had not taken hold in the early 1950s, so drug-related violence was not as prevalent as in today's big cities. Patterson and I had no difficulty avoiding those pitfalls during our short stay, and went about our business without incident. In short order, we became invisible members of the community and wondered why it was easy. We were in. We drank, gambled, and visited nightclubs almost every day and night. For lovers of jazz, we had our choices in Chicago. Establishments such as the Club DeLisa and the Brass Rail were favorites for top-name live entertainment. I always brought back to Cleveland the latest dance craze, and what we learned in Chicago was no exception. I recall a hotel jukebox playing "Heartbreak Hotel", by a singer we did not know anything about. We prided ourselves in our knowledge of music and performers. Apparently he was new or at least not well known in our hometown. We purchased his record, took it back to Cleveland and introduced many of our friends to a youngster named Elvis Presley.

A long-term, deep-penetration type operation was not to be. We were recalled to our Cleveland post of duty. Maybe someone saw our travel vouchers and thought we were having too much fun. We probably were, but the end justifies the means, or so they say, and we were making tremendous progress toward our goal. Maybe too much progress. Our recall remains a mystery.

I look back on that first undercover assignment and wonder why we were not "burned" immediately upon arriving in Chicago. *Somebody* "up there" was looking out for us. There are certain characteristics that undercover agents must acquire or possess if they are to survive their rookie mistakes. One of the most important traits for success in the jungle is versatility. The ability to feel relatively comfortable and at home in almost any surroundings or situation is a must. There is a tendency for so-called undercover agents to feel that they are wearing their badge and credentials on their forehead. Many feel that even when they enter a crowded and noisy room all eyes turn to them and stare. Wrong.

I suppose my varied interests and hobbies paved the way for my entrée into many situations arising almost daily during my undercover assignments. I could discuss Brahms or Basie music; ASA 64 or ASA 400 film capabilities; recording music at 1 7/8 or 15 ips; backroom and alley gambling versus casino gambling, and equally important, during those undercover years I could literally "drink most people under the table." This is what I refer to as versatility.

As an undercover agent, it was necessary to take on many roles and be prepared for any eventuality. An inexperienced, clean-cut college type special agent, reminded me of the saying "an accident trying to find some place to happen." In my particular case, I became so intertwined in my role, that when I returned home, which was rare, I had difficulty responding to someone addressing me by my true name. One such humorous occasion occurred when I returned home and in assisting my wife with the household chores, I signed the checks to pay our monthly bills. Unfortunately, I signed the checks with my undercover name, but no lasting damage was done.

In defining the term "undercover" by law enforcement officials in the 1950s, one thought of an officer donning the attire of his adversaries for a few evening and weekends; becoming drinking buddies with the subjects and their friends; gathering the necessary evidence or information; and successfully concluding the investigation before the week was over. That's fine for a two-hour TV movie, but not in the real world. This myth was erroneously based on the assumption that similar racial and ethnic backgrounds overshadowed all other considerations.

In our hometown of Cleveland, Ohio, it was actually believed by some Service officials that Special Agents Owens and Patterson could don sport clothes, drive an unmarked government vehicle (no radio, armrests or ashtrays) into the city's ghetto, and in a very short time, consort with the underworld, and infiltrate their illegal numbers lottery operation all in the same day. Wrong again.

We were successful, but we did it our way. It was, and still is, wrong to assume that any race or ethnic group will accept "one of their own" simply because of racial or ethnic similarities. Those myths gradually declined insofar as being acceptable "modus operandi," because failures in the field by undercover agents were so commonplace.

Patterson and I learned early in our Intelligence Division careers that any success in the field must be based on some reason other than being "soul brothers." As we accumulated years of experience, including some failures along the way, we developed individual techniques that worked. On more than one occasion we were complimented by our adversaries after their trials and convictions with comments such as, "You guys missed your calling"; or "We could really use you fellas in our operation." I recall being offered a partnership by a professional photographer; of trading, loaning, and borrowing record albums from noted musicians; and being invited to sit in and compete in a chess tournament with serious chess players. As can be seen, Patterson and I always had a "gimmick" that almost guaranteed acceptance. It worked.

Chapter Five

Patterson and I returned to Cleveland from Chicago just in time to attend our first Intelligence Division school, which is now referred to as the Special Agents' Basic School(SABS), and held at the Glynco, Georgia training facility.

The class that Patterson and I attended in 1955 was conducted for special agents in the Central Region, comprising Ohio, Indiana, West Virginia, Virginia and Kentucky. The subject matter included all aspects of tax fraud; evidence and procedure; Federal Rules of Criminal Procedure; and emphasis on the criminal sections of the Internal Revenue Code (Title 26 USC), as well as appropriate sections of Title 18 USC violations.

Other training that was stressed included the various indirect methods of determining correct income. Taxpayers under criminal investigation are not required to furnish their books and records, nor can they be compelled to answer any questions that might tend to incriminate them, a right granted under the Constitution of the United States. It goes without saying that most taxpayers investigated by the Criminal Investigation Division avail themselves of their Fifth Amendment Rights. Appendix A-1 is a hypothetical, yet typical example of the manner in which investigations were conducted and role-playing by students attending SABS. It was stressed throughout the training that agents cannot expect taxpayers to cooperate and help the investigator develop a criminal case. We later found that to be an understatement.

Note: Reading Appendix A-1 would be very interesting at this juncture because it would furnish some insight into a special agent's daily activities that eventually become "routine."

Our SABS training lasted several weeks, after which were turned to our regular investigations.

Like other new special agents, Patterson and I were assigned regular fraud investigations, but seldom could we complete an investigation before we were called away on another undercover assignment. Our regular tax cases would have to await our return.

Our next undercover assignment came shortly after our first schooling in Cleveland. We were called to the Regional Office in Cincinnati and learned during a briefing our assignment involved Newport, Kentucky, a town across the Ohio River from Cincinnati, and a racketeer stronghold. Casino gambling dens, big-name entertainment, brothels, and police and politicians on the pad. A very prosperous little town. A former governor of Kentucky is reported to have said that Newport had a right to be dirty if it wanted it that way. They wanted it that way. Naturally, the clergy wanted it otherwise. In 1956 our subject, Frank Andriola, known locally as "Screw" Andrews, had been charged with the murder of his competitor, numbers operator Melvin Clark. He successfully pleaded self-defense shortly before our arrival.

Andrews' arrest record dated back to 1923. He had a reputation of coming out unscathed from personal confrontations with competitors and local authorities. We were advised that he, as well as his associates, politicians and police friends, were dangerous. We were young and gung-ho, and unmoved about possible dangers, because we were federal agents just like in the movies. Specifically, we were to infiltrate several casino-type clubs in Newport, Kentucky that catered to African-Americans, but were owned by the infamous "Screw Andrews," a name he acquired not out of affection, but by the manner in which he treated those around him. All of the illegal clubs controlled by "Screw" Andrews were on Central Avenue in Newport, around the corner from the police department. As a matter of fact, when traffic congestion became so great during the peak periods (all night long) at the clubs, the police department assigned officers to direct traffic. We were again cautioned about our lives being in jeopardy if our identities were learned, and to exercise extreme caution in gathering the necessary evidence for "probable cause" for search and/or arrest warrants, relating to the numbers lottery and coin-operated gaming devices. In 1956, under federal law, all lottery operators and their writers were required to purchase a $50 federal gambling stamp. All coin-operated gaming devices, such as one-armed bandits, required a $250 gambling stamp, and such gambling stamps were required to be prominently displayed on the premises. At that time federal law permitted the names of the purchasers of the gambling stamps to be made public and available to local police officials. Such names were prominently listed in local newspapers. The Supreme Court eventually declared making public the names of the purchasers unconstitutional.

As wide open as the clubs appeared to be, Patterson and I were advised that the trained eye of the doorman at each of these establishments was watching all persons approaching the establishments, the principal one of which was the Sportsman's club. Others had tried to enter in the past and were unsuccessful, but they had been Caucasian. We were told that the FBI had made an attempt to raid the club, but underestimated the strength of the doors and were unsuccessful in gaining entry. The FBI agents hastily visited the nearby fire station to borrow axes, but were denied their use. Their request, according to fire department officials, was "highly irregular." This story was related to Patterson and me to illustrate the hostility of Newport toward any and all outsiders, particularly law enforcement.

Patterson and I had to devise an original and unsuspecting approach to gaining entry. Having had a certain amount of undercover experience in Chicago, we decided that in the future we would call the shots and refused to venture to Cincinnati, Ohio or Newport, Kentucky, until the possibility of our identities being discovered was reduced to a minimum. Through one of our contacts, we obtained "undercover" license plates for our personal car and driver's license in fictitious names. We did not realize it at the time, but the undercover license plates were "hot," that is, they were furnished from a specific series that would be readily identified by most law enforcement personnel. We recall being followed and greeted by unmarked police cars in distant cities. We immediately discarded the plates and obtained another set, resorting to our own devices. That problem was solved. We personally had to resolve many such problems during our undercover careers.

Patterson and I had other problems. We were supposed to use our personal funds, so we refused to depart without funds with which to operate. Apparently, the Cleveland District was not familiar with a procedure whereby travel funds could be advanced to agents to cover expenses while in a travel status. Somehow the district office found sufficient funds for us to pay for our lodging, food, gambling, and meet our other immediate needs.

The Cincinnati hotel where we decided to stay during our assignment had a dining room and a jukebox with the latest rhythm and blues records, with which we were familiar. The dining room waitresses enjoyed the music and my first thought, Bingo! They did not know it, but they would be our entrée into the clubs across the Ohio River in Newport, Kentucky.

As I recall, the jukeboxes would play six selections for a quarter. It took all of two or three dollars in quarters that evening to direct our conversation with the waitresses toward live entertainment and gambling. The girls joyously suggested visiting the Sportsman's Club after they finished their shift at the hotel. We were assured that getting into the clubs would be no problem because we would be with them. We accepted their offer with assurances from them that being strangers would not create any problems. We spent all night at the Sportsman's Club, except for short visits to the other two clubs on the same street. Both Patterson and I won varying amounts from the slot machines known as one-armed bandits, and we also bet on the numbers. We gambled at the blackjack and dice tables and had a sufficient amount of luck to impress our escorts. We observed the drawing of the winning lottery numbers and listened to the constant ringing of the telephones. We overheard persons on the telephone giving out the winning numbers just drawn. We had heard enough, and participated in gambling activity sufficient to establish probable cause for all three clubs that first evening. We subsequently visited all three clubs without our first escorts on many other evenings, gathering additional data and information. We also placed wagers on the illegal lottery with writers at the hotel, and at several locations throughout Cincinnati. We asked the writers if we had to be present at the Sportsman's Club to receive our money if we hit the numbers. They said, "No, we'll bring the money to you." Before we departed, there were writers looking for us before they turned in their work for the day, because they received a commission on their book. We were big-time spenders and popular. We could afford to be, as we were spending our nightly gambling winnings.

At the clubs, we placed invisible-to-the-eye markings on all of the one-armed bandits, dice tables, and other gambling equipment, for future identification. It was fortunate that the clubs did not have black or purple lights because as we learned later, everything bearing the invisible-to-the-eye markings would have lighted up like a Christmas tree, including our hands and clothing.

It was not known at the time, but the one-armed bandits could be recessed in the wall and not visible to the public during daylight hours. I believe that this was noted in our Affidavit of Probable Cause for the search warrants. The recessed walls were located during the raid, which, incidentally, was highly successful. The raid resulted in a Cincinnati newspaper's headlines on May 25, 1956:

"T-Men Seize 26 Slots in Newport. Three Places Hit by
Agents. Two Men Arrested on Tax Counts. Similar Action
is Taken in Eight Other Cities At Same Time."

Another Cincinnati newspaper carried a similar article on the same day.
It read,

'Panels No Secret to Federal Agents. 27 Slots Seized.
Casino Active Despite Raids.".

Frank "Screw" Andrews was one of the persons arrested.

Following the raid, attorneys for the defendants vigorously attempted
to identify the special agents who signed the Affidavits for Probable Cause,
but to no avail. It was rumored that the FBI had paid informants, who
signed the affidavits as special agents, and Andrews' attorney thought that
the warrants were faulty because of possible misrepresentations. However
no one was completely convinced of this misrepresentation and "Screw"
Andrews, through his underworld connections, found out from a source in
the IRS in Cleveland that there were two recently hired African-American
special agents, i.e., Owens and Patterson, in that district's Intelligence
Division.

When we learned of this IRS employee's underworld connections, we
seriously considered taking matters in our own hands and eliminating
this menace to our well-being. My first thought was to leave this person
in his car one evening in a lonely place with his head in his hands. A
cooler head prevailed, and Patterson, the ever-cautious attorney, suggested
that we first discuss the matter and our options with the person involved,
and if he gave us a hard time, then we "make him an offer he could not
refuse." It was well-known in the city's subcultures that Patterson and I
were street fighters, and our one and only offer would leave this person
with few alternatives. One evening after work we followed him to his car
and discussed the matter. He resigned from the Service shortly thereafter,
and our paths never crossed again. "Screw" Andrews later pleaded guilty
to the occupational tax stamp violation, and was sentenced to one year
in the federal penitentiary. Patterson and I, and the courts, would have
another encounter with Andrews five years later—same night clubs—same
agents—same violations—same "Screw" Andrews, plus some of his
cohorts.

However, it was not until our next undercover assignment in the Greater Cincinnati area we learned of the dangers involved when working in Newport, and "Screw" Andrews as our target. For the time being that was not our problem. That would come later.

Chapter Six

Lest one get the impression that our assignments were restricted to working undercover, Patterson and I carried a full workload of income tax investigations back in our home district, the same as other agents in the division. This did not pose any particular problem for me insofar as promotions were concerned, because for reasons I could not fathom, I had an impressive prosecution record in my group. My then supervisor, having been highly successful in criminal cases, likened me to him in his earlier years in the field. He commented, "We stumble blindly in our ignorance with only our goals in mind, and ignore the little obstacles that others seem to magnify." He promoted me at every opportunity. He had been the most outspoken official when I was initially interviewed for the special agent position, and it was apparent to me that he had become my mentor.

One of my first income tax investigations comes to mind, which involved a small grocer, who omitted more than ninety percent of his gross receipts from his tax return, business Schedule C. Unfortunately for him, an alert Internal Revenue Agent noted that the purchases, inventory, and expenses were not in line with a typical business of that type and referred the case to the Intelligence Division. It was subsequently assigned to me as a joint investigation with the Audit Division. Our first objective was to obtain the taxpayer's books and records relating to income that would accurately reflect his gross receipts. If his receipts could be proven, it would weigh heavily in establishing willful intent, a necessary element in criminal tax cases. Even without such evidence, the revenue agent and I concluded that the grocer's provable 'net worth' and expenditures increased substantially each year. When the taxpayer, his accountant and his attorney were confronted with of our preliminary findings, i.e., that the taxpayer's wealth (net worth) increased substantially each year under investigation, while his reported income was minimal, they reluctantly turned over the accurate books and records. That was one of the several mistakes they made. If anyone plans to cheat on paying taxes, they should

(1) never maintain two sets of books, (2) use a tin can to bury the money in the backyard instead of accumulating bank accounts, and acquiring assets, (3) never try to keep up with the Joneses next door, and finally, (4) keep their scheme a secret. We in IRS have been so successful in the past because tax evaders are also human beings with human frailties, who cannot keep secrets. In our free society, even tax evaders wish to establish respectability in their communities. That requires breaking some of the cardinal rules that successful cheaters must adhere to. Very few individuals can keep a secret indefinitely. They must tell someone, and therein lies their vulnerability. In the case cited above, the taxpayer broke all the rules for successful cheating; i.e., he told his accountant to use the fictitious set of books ; he lived in a well-to-do neighborhood; drove a late model car; accumulated sizable bank accounts; and maintained a lifestyle that, while not extravagant, could not be considered frugal. Gathering this information during the investigating was routine, and the taxpayer subsequently pleaded guilty to four counts of income tax evasion. My supervisor stated that both he and the division chief were pleasantly surprised at the outcome of the case. Originally, they considered the criminal potential in the case to be minimal at best. They thought this specific item/net worth-type case would be good training ground for a rookie special agent and an even more recently hired internal revenue agent. I always felt that my facial expression at that time made them wonder if they had made a mistake in selecting me for a special agent position. One of them much later jokingly stated that, "Hilton doesn't want you wasting his time on Mickey Mouse cases." After my obvious displeasure in receiving a practice case, I do not recall a similar occurrence during my years in the Cleveland District under three different supervisors.

Chapter Seven

Sometime in the fall of 1956, Patterson and I were again advised that our undercover services were needed. This time it was in the Miami area. We used my personal vehicle with undercover license plates and drivers' licenses with aliases. I recall that between the two of us we had less than $500. With each of us having a wife and three children, we lived from paycheck to paycheck and there was no excess of household funds to use for undercover purposes. His small sum was to last us at least until we submitted expense vouchers at the end of the month. To make matters even worse, we were told to travel to New Orleans and assist the Intelligence Division for a few days before going to Miami. Our $486 seemed smaller.

It was 1956, even before equal opportunity in housing, so we obtained a copy of *Ebony* magazine, that listed the hotels, motels, and rooming houses, where African-Americans could find food, and overnight lodging. *Ebony* published a list of such places each year in one of their monthly publications. Thanks to *Ebony*, you saved us some grief on more than one occasion.

While planning the trip, I kidded Patterson, "You're a country boy, how do we get to New Orleans from Cleveland without going through Mississippi?" He replied, "You don't. On this trip we'll take our pocket commissions, gold badges, and our .38s." The .38s Patterson referred to were our .38 caliber long-barrel revolvers, which, to say the least, were very menacing. We advised ours superiors that we might die in the Deep South, but we would not spend one night in one of their jails. As we crossed the Tennessee state line and headed further south, I had that strange feeling of impending danger. My premonition was right. An incident was just over the horizon.

We were not only two African-Americans ripe for the whims of some greedy deputy sheriff or gas station cowboy, but we were traveling with Ohio license plates. I don't think that any Northerner, whether African-American or white, with Ohio, Illinois, or New York plates would have been welcome in the Deep South in the 1950s.

Less than two hours into the heartland of the south, we passed a vehicle parked on the side of the road, with a white male, in uniform, in the driver's seat. CB'ers would now refer to that situation as "Smokey wrapped in a brown paper bag, taking pictures." Within a mile or so the vehicle overtook us and stopped diagonally across the road, causing us to also stop. He approached our vehicle, looked inside and advised that we were speeding.

He asked us to get out of the car.

I asked, "How fast were we going?"

He replied, "As fast as I say you were going, nigger."

"This is it," I told Patterson.

"Right, you wearing your piece?" he responded. "Let's take him, or our travel through Mississippi will be short-lived."

The officer overheard our entire conversation and stood by the vehicle motionless. We departed our vehicle from both sides, with our gold badges pointed at him and our hands on our revolvers that were in full sight.

"Who the hell are you guys," he asked.

"Feds, and keep your hands in full sight. Where's your station," we asked.

"About four miles back, but there's no need to contact them. It was all a mistake."

We emptied his revolver, and returned both revolver and bullets to him. We suggested that he relay a message to his superiors and comrades, "Do not—with us." He must have relayed the message, because just before we crossed the state line, we observed a marked police car with an occupant, who waved.

I asked Patterson, "What if we were just a couple of guys going to Biloxi to visit relatives?"

"Guess," he responded.

We continued our journey to New Orleans, thankfully without further incident. The details of our stay in New Orleans eludes me, but Special Agent Naurbon L. Perry had Patterson and me placing illegal bets with an extremely hard-to-reach bookie in the downtown area. He was reputed to accept bets only from persons with whom he was acquainted. We had no difficulty in changing his mind. What money will do to greedy people.

I also recall eating plenty of seafood, prepared various ways. It was also my first encounter with mouth-watering bouillabaisse. The seafood alone was reason enough for me to volunteer to work in New Orleans, but they were not ready for African-Americans special agents in that city in 1956. Pat and I had trouble with the coffee, served black and thick. I also remember learning the tango in a school gym. I believe that our guides, two African-American police officers, were responsible for me learning the dance. Patterson sat it out. He had two left feet when it came to dancing. We moved on to Miami after our short stay in New Orleans. I had hoped that someday I would surprise my family and friends and win some dance contest doing the tango. The opportunity never came.

Upon arrival in Miami, we drove to a hotel/motel establishment that we probably learned of from *Ebony* magazine or word of mouth. We rented an efficiency suite in an apartment-motel on a monthly basis that was frequented by top-name African-American entertainers. Our first morning there we observed ballad singer Roy Hamilton, who was recuperating from an illness. Later in the day we saw blues-belting *"Everyday I've got the Blues,"* singer Joe Williams; and vibe-playing Lionel Hampton. I told Patterson, "Man, we've died and gone to heaven." Insofar as the assignment was concerned, we met with our contact person, at his home in Coral Gables. I'm not certain, but I think that he had a African-American gardener, and Patterson and I suggested meeting elsewhere in the future. We had no difficulty placing bets with various writers and furnishing general gambling intelligence to our contact man regarding numbers (bolita) writers, their vehicles, license numbers, and times of pickup.

A person with whom we became friendly, who introduced us to various lottery writers laughingly stated, "Don't you guys get my writers in trouble."

"Trouble, from us. The only trouble he'll get from us is if he don't pay us when we hit Bolita."

Patterson and I developed a routine wherein one of us bet with a particular writer and the other remained outside to get the description of the vehicle, license plate and the time of the writer's departure. We advised our contact man not to set up surveillance in the area, because the agents would be "burned" almost immediately. He complied. We mailed detailed daily memorandums of our activities to our contact man, rather than visit his home. Patterson and I were not happy that on our first visit to our contact man's home, the gardener gave us more than a casual look.

We spent several months in Miami, and developed a taste for CuttySark scotch and a Cuban rum, and more southern cooking. An airman stationed in Miami made frequent trips to Cuba with the plane crew and liquor was brought back, sometimes almost filling the nose of the plane. The airman joked about one occasion that the plane was so laden with booze that the takeoff had to be aborted, but without mishap. Pat and I also learned how to make fancy rum drinks when money was low and we had exhausted our scotch supply. From time to time we were asked questions when we were separated, which, on the surface, seemed innocent enough, but we knew otherwise. Someone was interested in our past, present, and future. As we learned much later, we need not have worried, as far as the undercover assignment was concerned. That is another story that will be discussed later. Our contact man advised us that shortly we would be moving on to Fort Lauderdale, Dania, or Pompano Beach, so we should get our "gotta-move-on" story circulating.

I recall seeing posters in barbershops, taverns and on fences that announced the arrival of blues-singer B.B. King, for a concert just outside of Miami. He was then known as Blues Boy, and had been a disk jockey, but was now belting out the blues. I suggested to Patterson that we attend the concert. At first he declined, being a lover of big bands, Count Basie, Ella Fitzgerald, and the supper club set. I was more versatile. I enjoyed Patterson's type of music, but I also enjoyed the blues, even back in my childhood days.

As a youngster, I recall my mother saying to me, "You're not old enough to know what the blues is all about. Where did you get that record?"

I always teased her and retorted, "Listen to the words, it's great. This is music."

> "I've had my fun,
> If I don't get well no more
> My health is failing me
> and I'm going down slow.
> Please write my mother.
> Tell her the shape I'm in."

Before the song ended, my mother left the room. She had a saying: "Hilton, you'll never live to be sixteen." When I made sixteen, she was certain I would not live to see twenty-one. At nineteen when I departed for the military, she gathered my favorite records and put them away. So wanting to see and hear B.B. King was just a natural thing for me. Patterson relented, and accompanied me to the concert near Opa Locka, outside of Miami. That was his undoing. While we were on the road on other assignments, he would sit for hours and listen to my tape recordings of B.B. King, Bobby "Blue" Bland, Dinah Washington and "Cousin" Ray Charles. He always claimed that he listened to my music because he was bored and had nothing else to do. Somehow, after a hard day in the streets and needing something to quiet the nerves he suggested-insisted on listening to some of my favorites. That suited me just fine. In later years, and even now, whenever I heard B.B. King singing "Sweet Sixteen," I'd think of Patterson and that night in Opa Locka, when B.B. King opened his show with that tune. Even today, there are songs that are reminders of Patterson and me in other places, such as Boston, Memphis, Little Rock, Cincinnati, Newport, and Chattanooga.

The time for our departure from Miami came, and without fanfare, we moved on to Fort Lauderdale and into gambling circles without any problems. Our friends in Miami saw to that. This was another example of us being fully accepted in two communities (Miami and Fort Lauderdale) and officials somewhere in IRS unable to see the benefits that could be derived from long-range, deep-penetration type assignments. We made our usual excuses for departing, and returned to Cleveland in time for Christmas, 1956.

Chapter Eight

Shortly after returning from our 'experience' in Miami, Patterson departed for Washington, D.C., to attend the Treasury Law Enforcement Officers' Training School.

We had, up until then, always traveled together. He was surprised when he telephoned me at home one evening and learned that I had not been scheduled for the same class. I attended the same school about six months later. The school and training are described in detail in Appendix A-2.

However, in Cleveland, I finally had an opportunity to work on cases in my home district that I had long neglected.

One of my earlier successful prosecution cases involved a schoolteacher and her attorney husband. This case originated with information received from an anonymous source who was angry with the attorney. I am not sure if I finished this case before departing on another undercover assignment. I was constantly being criticized by taxpayers for my delays and sudden disappearances, but I somehow completed the cases before we had a statute of limitations problem. Criminal cases had a six-year period from the filing of returns or the due date of returns in which criminal proceedings could be instituted. There is no statute of limitations on civil fraud.

The schoolteacher-attorney, husband and wife case went to trial in 1959. A local Cleveland newspaper wrote:

Attorney, Wife Fined $10,000 in Tax Dodge. An attorney and his school-teacher wife agreed to plead guilty to tax evasion, but the wife had a change of heart when appearing before the Court. She advised the judge that, "I had no intention of defrauding the Government." The judge stated, "Then I will have to refuse a guilty plea and let the jury decide."

Earlier, a local newspaper reported the incident in an article that stated, "Wife Foils Plan in Tax Case."

However, not long after this incident, the wife had another change of heart; the attorney-husband pleaded guilty and the wife was found guilty by the court; and each was fined and placed on probation. The only thing that stands out in my mind about this case was the fact that the schoolteacher-wife treated this special agent, and her attorney-husband, as if they were elementary school children in her classroom, who needed her ruler across their knuckles or backside. I was hoping she would display a similar attitude toward the sentencing judge, but she was relatively quiet, which means she knew whom she could bully.

The cases cited here are not necessarily in chronological order, but are shown to illustrate the types of cases handled by agents on a daily basis. Another of my cases that drew newspaper coverage involved a local physician. After his guilty plea to attempted income tax evasion, a newspaper article stated,

"Doctor Escapes Jail in Tax Case"

I recall this prosecution case in 1962 when I investigated a physician who subsequently pleaded guilty to income tax evasion. The court, in imposing sentence, noted that: "Dr. _____ works 15 to 18 hours a day serving his patients and probably doesn't keep very good books." Judge _____ said his court had never encountered "anyone who feels greater remorse than Dr._____." He was ordered to pay back taxes and placed on probation.

Other successful prosecution cases in my home district followed for me, and undercover assignments because even more frequent. The names Patterson and Owens became household words in the IRS intelligence community, and we were constantly on the go. We were too tired to be worried, frightened, or concerned about the nature of our next assignment. We knew that it would be the same thing all over again. More drinking, gambling, and betting on the numbers or horses. The cities, hotel rooms, food, and even people, all began to look the same to us. Sometime during the late1950s, Patterson's first wife died, leaving him with three small children. With the help of relatives caring for his children, he was able to continue working undercover around the country. The work was no longer exciting for either of us. Patterson was no longer the jolly guy I once knew, but that was understandable with the loss of his wife and relatives looking after his children. It was truly time for us to "come in from the cold." I should have insisted, but I didn't, for fear of being accused by Pat of attempting to run his life. Regrettably, not insisting was a fatal mistake.

At this writing I am having difficulty identifying specific years, and dates of events. On one occasion, when Patterson and I were both back in our home district, I received a telephone call from an IRS co-worker who wanted me to relay a message to Patterson. The telephone conversation was as follows,

> Larry: "How you doing, Hilt."
> Hilton: "Fine Larry, what's up."
> Larry: "I don't think it's a secret anymore. Weren't you and Patterson working in Miami a while back using aliases?
> Hilton: "Who's asking?"
> Larry: "I attended a dance over the weekend, and met a girl from Miami, who is looking for Curtis. She traced you guys to Cleveland."
> Hilton "I know who you're talking about. Did she say why she's looking for him?"
> Larry: "What makes the world go around—love. Tell Curtis to call me when he returns. I'll be here the rest of the day."
> Hilton: "Right, Larry. I'll tell him, and thanks."

She mentioned to our co-worker that she had met Patterson and his buddy while they were "working" in Miami. She went on to state that when she and Patterson were alone, his manner changed and she was able to discern that he was highly educated in business and law. She surmised that he was a professional and being from out-of-state, he must be a "fed." With Ohio license plates, it would not be difficult to find out the rest if she came to Cleveland.

Upon arriving, she immediately learned that Patterson and Owens fit the description of those two "playboys" that had visited Miami in 1956, We later learned that those innocent questions being asked about us while we were in Florida were for her personal benefit. She was suspicious, but not being part of the gambling fraternity, she did not relate her suspicions to others. Suffice it to say that Patterson and the young lady got together, talked over old times, and subsequently married. But things did not work out and they were eventually divorced. Being married to a federal agent who spends the greater part of his life working undercover cannot be handled by most wives. She, like so many others, could not handle it. In all fairness to her, and the many other wives in her category, they should not be required to handle it. Years later when I had an official say in the matter, I strongly opposed selecting married men for long-term undercover assignments. As I look back over the years, I cannot help but wonder whether a lot of the undercover agents would still be married to their first wives if they had refused to work undercover on the long-term assignments.

Chapter Nine

The early 1960s were turbulent years in government and elsewhere. Patterson and I were still being "shuffled" around the country. Attorney General Robert F. Kennedy was making his presence felt by emphasizing an all-out war on organized crime. For most of his career, J. Edgar Hoover, director of the Federal Bureau of Investigation, denied the existence of organized crime, the Mafia or La Cosa Nostra.

However, high-ranking federal government officials decided in 1961 that Newport, Kentucky, a longtime racketeer stronghold, should be the target of the all-out effort to rid that city of gambling, prostitution and less-than-savory police and elected officials. There were many who considered Attorney General Robert Kennedy to be naïve. They were wrong.

In that same year, Special Agent Patterson and I learned that we had volunteered once again to work undercover in the Greater Cincinnati Area, which included Newport and Covington, Kentucky. In the same manner as five years earlier, Frank "Screw" Andrews was again our target. However, at the initial meeting, we asked for a complete rundown on "Screw Andrews" and Newport, Ky. We got it.

Newport had not changed. "Screw" Andrews was still top dog in the eyes of the public. In the late 1950s the clergy in Newport campaigned vigorously in Newport for reform. By the early 1960s the reform movement had enough momentum to run former NFL quarterback, George Ratterman, for sheriff.

The U.S. Senate Rackets Committee was conducting hearings on gambling and had subpoenaed many northern Kentucky gambling figures to testify in Washington. There was a move to separate a Circuit Court judge and a Campbell County grand jury that was investigating reports of vice payoffs. Witnesses were testifying before a federal grand jury in Lexington, Kentucky, about gambling and vice, and the Newport Police Chief was facing ouster action. That was the Newport to which Patterson and I had returned.

While still a candidate seeking office, Ratterman was duped into purportedly meeting a casino operator turned informant. They met in a downtown Cincinnati hotel room. At the hotel Ratterman was drugged and taken across the river to a Newport hotel room. By coincidence, Newport police found him in bed with a naked stripper. He was arrested on prostitution charges. It was rumored that his clothes were removed and he was taken to the Newport police station wrapped in a sheet or blanket.

In the well-publicized trial that followed, he proved that he was framed and the case was dismissed. This incident did not surprise the public, and the clergy found new strength in their drive for reform. They suddenly had unexpected help—Attorney General Robert F. Kennedy.

The Attorney General ordered a full-scale war on organized crime in Newport. Frank "Screw" Andrews and his Sportsman's Club were the targets. Andrews was reputed to be a front for "Trigger" Mike Coppola, who was in semiretirement in Miami, but was also reputed to still control the numbers racket in Harlem.

According to newspaper accounts, Andrews was right for the job in Newport. His arrest record dated back to the early 1920s. Andrews was greatly feared in the Greater Cincinnati area. His one-year stint in the federal penitentiary in 1956 for gambling tax violations did not seem to have any effect on his method of operation at the clubs.

Patterson and I set up "light housekeeping" at a hotel outside of downtown Cincinnati, and immediately made contact with numbers writers involved in the Newport operation. To the writers, we were hooked, as we displayed our schemes for picking the winning numbers on which we bet heavily. We played so many numbers with so many people, we had to win sooner or later. We lost more than we won, but writers never mentioned our losses, they only commented to others how much we were winning. While going through these exercises in Cincinnati, we were formulating our plans to hit Newport with a bang.

By this time we had developed some sophistication in the undercover game, so gaining entry into the Sportsman's Club should have posed no problem to professionals such as ourselves. Wrong.

The club had moved to the old location of the Alibi Club Electronically controlled steel doors with peepholes had been installed, and they permitted the inside attendant to view all persons attempting to enter. We were prepared for that eventually. Greed creates laxity, and in our case, the club welcomed persons who appeared ready and willing to part with the green stuff on the gambling tables, with the "ladies of the night," and the numbers lottery. In pimps' clothing, and a fistful of greenbacks, we had no difficulty finding suitable escorts. We also visited the Sportsman's Club in the company of our writers-friends from Cincinnati. There was never a lack of escorts to minimize our conspicuousness, if it ever existed.

The club resembled any Las Vegas casino, except the one-armed bandits could be recessed in the walls during daytime non-use. We focused our attention on obtaining evidence that persons did not have to be present at the drawing to collect their winnings. It was the club owner's (Andrews) contention that all persons had to be present to win, which would relieve him from liability for the federal tax on wagering. He also contended that there were no gaming devices on the premises. We obtained sufficient probable cause for search warrants, but lacked the evidence to implicate our main target, i.e., "Screw" Andrews as a principal in the operation. We were reminded that the Department of Justice wanted as airtight case on Andrews before any raid.

Tragedy struck. Special Agent Patterson suffered a near-fatal highway crash en route to his home in Cleveland, Ohio. He subsequently recovered, but insofar as the Newport undercover assignment was concerned, I had to go it alone, which posed no problem for me, except I had no one to watch my back. I had to continually justify to myself that my mission was worthwhile even though the special agents back in Cleveland went home to their wives and children each evening, and we still received the same pay. Something was very wrong, but I continually told myself to hang in there.

As a nightly visitor to the Sportsman's Club I struck up an acquaintance with well-known ballad singer Charles Brown, who was famous almost everywhere, except at the Sportsman's Club, where he was merely a fill-in during intermission for the main entertainer. On many occasions we discussed his earlier years, his famous million-seller record, known to us old-timers as *Drifting Blues*. Brown never discussed why he was trapped in the Sportsman's Club and I did not pry.

I had become almost a fixture at the club and on occasion I assisted in the drawing of the nightly numbers. It was during these periods of casual conversations with the club's master of ceremonies and other persons involved with "Screw" Andrews, that comments were made. Such comments in and of themselves were innocent, but when combined with statements and actions by others, a pattern could be discerned that definitely established Frank "Screw" Andrews as the principal. At this point, hasty preparations were made to raid the clubs. My voluminous daily memoranda were reviewed, discussed and used to prepare the all-important Affidavit for Probable Cause for the search warrant. Even I was surprised (and delighted) at the specificity and detail in my memoranda.

As preparations were made for the raid I always got that "what if there is a leak" complex. I was still visiting the clubs nightly and gathering evidence that would be used in my affidavit and any suspicion would have bought me six feet of ground. Obviously, there were no leaks.

A target date and time were set. More than 35 special agents from throughout the region were assembled, given their respective assignments, and briefed by me as to the interior of the club. The timing of the raid was to be exactly11:30 p.m., when the numbers lottery drawing would be in full progress. I breathed a sigh of relief when I learned that my dependable friend Special Agent Richard "Dick" Cotner, from our Toledo office, would plan and lead the raid. There is an old saying that, "If anything can go wrong, it will." That saying could certainly apply to an operation of the magnitude and importance of the Newport raid. Cotner was a bottom-line, no-nonsense person. My type of guy. Nothing went wrong that evening, but knowing Cotner, he had prepared for any eventuality. It was decided that exactly 11:30 p.m. I would be sitting at the bar near the electronic door, which I would open at precisely 11:30, and all I wanted to see was a bunch of familiar faces, all wearing gold badges with revolvers drawn.

Despite all of my undercover experience, that evening at the club was almost frightening. I thought of all the things that could go wrong and the ankle holster and weapon I wore that evening were no consolation. I felt like everyone was watching me as though I wore my gold badge on my forehead. I said to myself time and again, "Stop acting like a green kid just out of undercover school on your first assignment." I eventually calmed down as the evening wore on, music and dancing commenced, and the liquor freely flowed. I tried to convince myself, "Just another night, at least until 11:29, and thirty seconds, then worry." A group of Shriners, who were having a convention in Cincinnati, descended on the Sportsman's Club that evening and were fascinated with the Las Vegas atmosphere in such a small town. "H Hour" (11:30p.m.) had almost arrived. As it happened, I heard a banging at the door about thirty seconds too soon.

"Screw Andrews" nephew and I had a footrace to the electronic door. I won.

Retired Supervisory Criminal Investigator, then Special Agent Richard D. Cotner, vividly recalled the raid that he organized and led. The memorandum prepared by Cotner related his recollection of the incident.

> "Sorry I can't remember more, but you know the mind is the second thing to go with age.
>
> Your friend as always,
> Dick C.

These are my recollections of events and incidences leading to the raid upon the Sportsman's Club premises, Newport, Kentucky, in the summer of 1961.

Unlike the plan of attack on organized crime that was so prevalent during the Kiefaufer hearings in the early 1950s, the Kennedy Administration chose an aggressive attack by first gathering evidence through the use of informants, undercover operations, and extensive analyses of records which showed a flow of cash between individuals believed to be involved in the organized crime throughout the United States.

The Kennedy Administration chose this means of aggressively targeting individuals who were reputed to be involved in organized crime as the Kiefaufer investigation targeted everyone who owned a "personal pool cue." The Kennedy Administration, under the direction of Attorney General Robert Kennedy, chose to first gather intelligence from various areas, and target those areas for aggressive investigation by various Federal investigative agencies. Once these areas were selected, they were set in priority form and manpower and funds were committed to an all-out investigation of individuals believed to be involved in committing crimes such as interstate gambling, labor racketeering, political corruption, narcotics, etc. Among the locations selected nationally was the Greater Cincinnati area which not only encompassed Cincinnati, Ohio and the Ohio side of the river but several communities of Northern Kentucky on the Kentucky side of the river. Kentucky was used as a home base for many gamblers in that it seemed to enjoy some protection by local and State authorities. These little, small communities such as Newport and

Covington were headquarters for these operations while the real money was taken from those who participated in gambling out of the very rich communities of Cincinnati and its surroundings.

In June of 1961, I, R. D. Cotner, Special Agent, Intelligence Division U. S. Treasury, Internal Revenue, stationed at Toledo, Ohio, was called to Cincinnati, Ohio, for an interview with the Acting Regional Commissioner, Intelligence, Tom McGovern, along with Chief, Intelligence, Eldon Myers, from Cleveland, Ohio. It was related that before a new target area for an organized crime project was commenced in the Greater Youngstown area to which I, (Cotner), would be assigned as the Special-Agent-in-Charge, I would assist Harold Seyller, Special-Agent-in-Charge of the Cincinnati project in preparation for a raid upon the Sportsman's Club at Newport, Kentucky. The raid was expected to go down sometime in July or August of 1961. I soon reported to Cincinnati and commenced reviewing administrative files of the identified Screw Andrews case and most particularly the daily reports of undercover operatives.

The Sportsman's Club was a large nightclub situated in Newport, Kentucky, in the flat flood plain adjacent to the Ohio River. The club had a capacity of upwards to 700-1000 people on any given evening. Not only did it have a lush bar and restaurant but it headlined entertainers from coast to coast. However, its main attraction was the operation of a casino which afforded gamblers all the action in which they cared to participate; everything from betting on numbers to playing blackjack and dice. As I reviewed the information from the undercover operatives, I soon learned that the Sportsman's Club, even though operated mostly by White owners, had a clientele that was African-American. Further investigation of the files revealed that the service had employed, for a considerable period of time, African-American undercover operatives.

One operative, especially suited for this kind of penetration, was Special Agent Hilton Owens, whose permanent post of duty was Cleveland, Ohio. Owens was known to me as we had attended some Service schools together. The reports of Owens were extremely well detailed, backed with documentation when possible, and particularly elaborated upon names and addresses of all participants and to what extent they were involved. After review of the daily reports of Special Agent Owens, there was little question in my mind that the U. S. Commissioner would surely grant a Search Warrant for the premises of the Sportsman's Club and not only that, support the service of the warrant at nighttime which, in the rules of criminal procedure, nighttime warrants require extra special information. Prior to setting up the assignments for the service of the Search Warrant, I met with Special Agent Owens at a noted downtown hotel, in Cincinnati. There, we covered all that had transpired in Owens' knowledge, and mapped a course of action which ultimately would lead over thirty-six special Agents to come into the premises of the Sportsman's Club at 11:30 p.m. on the night of _____1961.

With the assistance of Special Agent Owens, who, incidentally, was continuing his daily contacts at the Sportsman's Club and placing wagers, elaborate drawing of the entire premises of the Sportsman Club were made by Special Agent Owens. Areas of concern were highlighted and an index was set for spelling out certain agents who would be in charge of those areas and what was required of them.

As the time drew close to the raid date, there was concern about a smooth and quick entry into the business. Special Agent John Murphy, of Norfolk, Virginia, was temporarily assigned to the Greater Cincinnati project. Murphy was a big, impetuous guy who had played football at the University of Mississippi. In his mannerism, while chewing a cigar, it was his delight to grab a 16-20 pound sledgehammer, and with just a few blows, penetrate any large door. As Owens and I assessed the entrance way to the Sportsman's Club, which was a double theater type door allowing one side to go in and allowing the other side to go out with a bar, as required by most fire statutes, Owens determined that the doors were metal bound and backed with one-inch plywood bolted to the metal skin. Murphy, who would be accompanying me, who would have a Search Warrant to serve, advise that he would make short order of the entry door to the Sportsman's Club. Owens and I both knew what would happen to that sledgehammer going against a metal door backed with plywood. It would bounce like a rubber ball. The raid was continued to be planned and the night of the service of the warrant came. Thirty-six agents came into the parking lot in various degrees of order following my car. I went to the door and announced to the doorman, as required by the statute, that I was a Federal officer and that I had a Search Warrant for the premises. Murphy was standing off to my rear with a sledgehammer. The doorman had the door partially open when I had been talking to him. There was commotion inside the premises and I quickly stepped aside. The doorman ran away immediately, and the door closed without my knowledge. Murphy commenced to beat on the door. When Murphy beat on the door, that was a signal for Owens, who was already inside seated at the bar, to come out the exit door. Owens went out the exit door while Murphy was still beating on the entrance door. The agents assigned to grab that door missed it when it rebound from its hinges, and it closed shut unbeknownst to me. I ran inside believing that I was accompanied by at least thirty-six agents, jumped to the table, .38 drawn, and announced to everyone in attendance that we were Federal officers and had a Search Warrant. It so happened that week the Greater Cincinnati area was entertaining the African-American Shriner's of the Masonic Lodge and a lot of Lodge members were in attendance. The premise was particularly packed. As I stood on the top of the table, I soon realized that I was the only White man in the place. I looked around. I could still hear Murphy banging on the door with the 16-pound sledge. I then looked at a young fellow sitting at the table on which I was standing. With my .38, I motioned for him to get up very gently and go over to the door and open it. The young fellow did so. In the meantime all the dealers and employees of the club were quickly trying to gather evidence and destroy it, as later observed.

The thirty-six agents came on the premises and assumed their various positions and stations of responsibility. Some customers and employees were identified and held for questioning while others, who were obviously only patrons, were permitted to leave.

Had it not been for the detailed reports of Special Agent Owens much of that information would have been lost. Much of the information, it was learned, was the basis for the civil tax investigation which ran into the hundreds of thousands of dollars.

Affidavits were taken from critical employees and customers. These affidavits turned out to be the backbone of the civil and criminal case. The agents who had gone into the premises at 11:30 p.m. remained on those premises for over forty-eight hours examining witnesses and counting cash. Silver dollars were found dropped in the water tanks of many stalls of the ladies' rest room to be hidden. Waitresses had taken the money and hidden it there. A secret panel was found back in the office area adjacent to a slot machine room. The agents walked around the premises time and time again and talked to people. Owens, Cotner and Harold Seyller had been directing the activities of the various seizing agents on the identification of items seized under the warrant and to deal with questions of the press and also questions by attorneys of Screw Andrews and his partners. There was a large safe found in one area—there were several safes found. It was later determined that each combine, who were members of the partnership and had a certain piece of the action, maintained a safe there and kept their own records separately. There was one constructed corner that I had passed about two times every hour for about twenty-four hours and every time I looked into the closet and I considered the outside wall, something seemed to be wrong. The outside wall appeared to be longer than that of the respective closet depth. When I finally had time, I reasoned that there had to be something constructed in back of that area. Having a lot of experience with my granddad over the years in carpenter work, I set about making a thorough analysis of the closet space. The closet was a standard closet in which there were hung some jackets and a hat on the shelf. I took all of the items out of the closet and started to examine it thoroughly. I ran upon a strange piece of #12 wire about eight inches in length. It was looped over one of the coat hangers. That wire was bare on both ends by about ¼ of an inch. When taking that wire and examining the interior of the closet, I found scratch marks around two nail heads that were about two inches apart. When I laid that wire across those two nail heads, an electrical buzz was heard, next a click and a panel opened which revealed an interior closet of another safe and boxes of current play records for the numbers business.

It was with the detail that Special Agent Owens was able to assemble during a very long aggressive and dangerous undercover assignment that allowed the government to convict at least eight defendants who were principal gamblers in the Cincinnati area and whose financial assistance went throughout the United States to help bankroll other illegal activities. And in doing so, a great amount of civil tax was recovered just simply through the meticulous, courageous work of Special Agent Hilton Owens.

Of interest to note, during the Screw Andrews trial, one of the many witnesses was a local African-American man, a gambler, who just could not seem to stay out of the "sauce." He loved his booze and every day he reached his limits. That was a concern at the trial to get him early in the morning before he was inebriated, but it did not happen that way. He was seated outside with the witnesses and every now and then he came up missing. Every time he came back he seem a little more jovial. By the time early afternoon came, he was called to the witness stand. Witnesses before him who had anything important to say or we knew to be very knowledgeable of the huge syndicated gambling operation at Sportsman's

Club, upon advice of counsel, claimed their constitutional privilege afforded them under the Fifth Amendment of the Constitution of the United States. In so claiming that privilege, they read it from a card that had been prepared very painstakingly by their counsel so that the court knew what their claim was and had a perfect enunciation of the Fifth Amendment of the Constitution. When this jovial African-American numbers runner was called to the witness stand he smiled all the way up to taking the chair—crossed his legs and smiled at the judge and everyone in the audience. When asked who he was, he was not inebriated enough to know that he should not claim his privilege under the Fifth Amendment. He looked at the judge and very proudly stated, "I'z takes five." This brought everyone's attention to what he had just said. The judge rolled forward in his chair as did the prosecutor and defense attorneys and said, "What did you say" and he said, "I'z takes five". With that and with everyone having an understanding of what he was saying, it really brought the house down that he was claiming his privilege under the Fifth Amendment.

The raid plans were kept so secret that even the agents who were called in from outside districts to help serve the warrant were not informed until the last minute. They came to Cincinnati and were all brought into a large briefing room where pictures, diagrams, schematics of the premises, things to anticipate, and individuals to look out for were all discussed. Special Agents Bernard E. Thompson of Toledo, Ohio and Guy Weatherall of Columbus, Ohio, were paired to assist in a phase of accounting for funds in the casino area. On one occasion I passed through a woman's restroom about 4:00 or 5:00 in the morning and found Thompson and Weatherall each in a women's restroom stall seated on the commode counting silver dollars. Thompson looked up and advised me that he had remarked to Guy Weatherall earlier that had his wife told him forty-eight hours earlier that at five in the morning he would be seated across a commode in a ladies' john in a African-American gambling establishment with Guy Weatherall counting silver dollars, he would have sworn she was out of mind . . .

The August 23, 1961 issue of a Cincinnati newspaper carried the following headline:
"Final Blow to Newport Vice. U.S. Agents Raid Rackets Center, Seize Hidden Cash, Slots, Records."

Another newspaper carried similar headlines:
"U. S. Agents Raid Ky. Club. Six Men Arrested on Charge
of Failure to have Gambling Stamp."

Rumor had it that Special Agent Owens had spent the last five years undercover in the Cincinnati, Ohio area following the raid on the same club. As I recall, one of the few times I drew my weapon and came very close to using it happened shortly after the raid, and before I departed the area. A strange automobile with four male passengers occupants drove very close to the curb where I was walking and suddenly stopped the vehicle. While I was not in the Wyatt Earp category, in life-threatening situations there were very few persons that could clear the holster faster than myself. By the time the vehicle had come to a halt, I had my weapon pointed about six inches from the nose of the driver, and quietly asked him if he had a problem. I was frightened and would surely have shot the driver without hesitation had he, or any occupants in the vehicle, made any sudden moves. I then advised him in street talk that everyone in the vehicle understood, "drive on ___ ___." He did. I had no further problems.

Newport, Kentucky never really recovered from the raid. Naturally, gambling continued, but it was disorganized and fragmented, without anyone in full control.

On the day of the raid an Intelligence Division official in Washington, D.C., testifying before the Senate Rackets Committee regarding the Newport-Covington, Kentucky area, informed the committee that it was the major "layoff" bookie center in the nation. It was welcome news in Washington that the Newport raid was a success and the Attorney General was elated.

Following the raid, many areas in Newport resembled a ghost town and those involved in illegal activities followed the advice of some famous person who once said: "Go West, young man, go West." Many did. They relocated in Las Vegas, Nevada. Others moved on to Miami Beach.

Chapter Ten

With my identity now known, my usefulness in the Cincinnati area was at an end. I was reassigned to the Youngstown Organized Crime Drive (OCD) project. The city was known as "Bombsville, U.S.A." At that time there had been more than 50 racketeer-related bombings of racketeers' automobiles, including innocent children as victims. There was a standing joke at the time that it was difficult locating a dependable newspaper delivery boy because they earned much more by visiting the local racketeers' home each morning and starting their cars for them to ensure they had not been "wired." A sick joke.

My old buddy, now Special-Agent-in-Charge Dick Cotner headed this Youngstown project. Patterson had recuperated sufficiently to also be assigned to the project. Unfortunately, another undercover assignment came before we became firmly established in Youngstown and we were off and running again. Where?, West Virginia.

In June 1962, two Wheeling, West Virginia numbers operators were convicted in the first trials held in the nation under new federal anti-racketeering statutes. A Wheeling, West Virginia newspaper carried the following headline in the June 15, 1962 edition:

"_____ Gets Four Years in First Anti-Racket Case.

_____ Sentenced to 1 year."

These cases stemmed from a numbers lottery operation that carried across the Ohio-West Virginia state line, resulting in an interstate numbers operation. Special Agent Patterson and I, and a number of other agents, worked in undercover and surveillance roles to obtain probable cause for search and arrest warrants relating to an illegal interstate lottery operation.

Even to this day I have difficulties in understanding why it was business as usual with the number of strange vehicles and agents racing back and forth between Ohio and West Virginia, trying to keep numbers writers and pickup men under constant surveillance. Our vehicles were not police-type marked vehicles, but it would be generous to say that the cars were inconspicuous. For the most part they were old, stripped-down, no frills vehicles, some even bearing the remnants of mobile radio antennas. By today's standards, our mobile radios and hand-carried radio sets, would be considered crude and unreliable, with battery packs requiring recharging after only several hours. Nonetheless, our surveillance teams were remarkably successful, and we bet with writers both in Ohio and West Virginia.

Insofar as my recollection is concerned, during cross-examination at the trial I was asked if I had observed any numbers activity crossing the state line. It was a very simple question that I could not answer, and that was the crux of our case. However, on direct testimony, I had previously described the routes taken, landmarks observed, persons and vehicles involved. Shortly after being asked by the defense about defendants crossing states' lines, the federal judge interceded and stated that, 'The Court takes Judicial Notice that the agent crossed the state line. Change your (defense attorney) line of questioning." Before the trial ended there was a parade of special agents who took the witness stand and the outcome of the trial was never in doubt.

It was not long after this trial and convictions that interstate-type gambling cases were turned over to the Federal Bureau of Investigation, while wagering Excise Taxes and stamp taxes remained with the IRS Intelligence Division.

As undercover assignments tend to lose their preciseness in my mind's eye, I still vividly recall what should be long forgotten. For instance, I paid the huge sum of four dollars to a street hustler selling a hot three-record set of the "Nat King Cole Story" albums. It also contained a twenty-four-page pictorial and family story brochure, with Nat and his family, one of whom was a tiny little girl, who is now famous in her own right. The records, even now, are a delight to hear.

In addition to remembering a record album set, I also recall purchasing a clear liquid in a fruit-jar type container from a Wheeling, West Virginia liquor store. I cannot recall the proof, but on one occasion some of the liquor spilled on our hardwood floor at home and removed stain and varnish as it sizzled. I could describe my wife as sizzling also, as she observed this minor incident. When word spread that Hilton was home and had brought some acid-looking concoction from the hills, some of our neighborhood close friends came over to see the firewater, but considered it unfit for human consumption, except in fruit punch. How long it remained in our liquor cabinet I do not recall, but suffice it to say that it was never consumed straight, since it was at least 190 proof. When returning home I always attempted to bring back the latest dance craze from the area I had departed. West Virginia was no exception. On those lonely nights away from home or when things got a little rough out there in the jungle, I invariably thought of some humorous incident such as the incident with the 190 proof booze or teaching a new dance to our close neighbors.

Chapter Eleven

Following the Wheeling, West Virginia fiasco, I was advised that a trial date had been set for Frank "Screw" Andrews. That was in 1962. I met a young prosecutor from the Justice Department, William Lynch, who was lead trial attorney for the case. I still remember our many hours of preparation, and me on the witness stand while he skillfully guided me through my testimony. It was often necessary for me to refresh my recollection from the daily memoranda of activities I had submitted to my contact man during the undercover assignment. Mr. Lynch was, and still is, my idea of the consummate prosecutor. He certainly helped me. Thanks again, Bill. I have seen his name in the press many times since and I was never surprised at his successes.

When the trial started there were eight defendants who had been previously indicted, including Frank "Screw" Andrews, two of his nephews, and five others involved in the Newport numbers operations.

In cases of this type where an undercover agent obtained the necessary information or evidence and signed the Affidavit for Probable Cause, the defense's initial thrust is to discredit the evidence or the agent, or both, and prove that there was insufficient probable cause for instance of the warrants. If they were to be successful in this endeavor the Court would suppress all evidence obtained during the raid as "fruits of the poison tree."

As far as the Sportsman's Club was concerned, the first hurdle for the prosecution was to prove that there was no entrapment and all statements made by me in the affidavit were true, accurate and sufficient.

Truth does not come in degrees and has never been a debatable subject for me. There are old sayings that "You can't be a little pregnant, or a little dead." I further contend that one cannot be a little untruthful. It is all or nothing. In the instant case, I felt absolutely secure in the fact that my testimony could not be shaken, because my daily memoranda set forth a true and complete chronology of my activities during my numerous visits to the club. At the outset of the trial the court separated the witnesses. That is, anyone required to testify at the trial was not permitted in the courtroom during proceedings until such time as they had completed their testimony and were excused by the Court.

Prior to the trial date, I had reviewed my memoranda hour after hour until I had memorized many of the documents almost verbatim. I was ready, at least for direct testimony.

Government prosecutor Bill Lynch seemed to carry me through the testimony with ease, from the time Patterson and I were notified of the assignment, up to and including the night of the raid. I cannot recall how long or how many days I was on the witness stand, but the numerous and constant objections from the defense attorneys did not seem to impress the court, which constantly overruled the defense's objections. Incidentally, the defendants had three attorneys who took notes, which they constantly exchanged. I knew trouble was on the horizon. Eventually my direct testimony was concluded. That was only the beginning.

It is also blurred in my memory how long I was on the witness stand. My preparation for the trial did not prepare me for the onslaught yet to come. It reminded of the mock trial at one of our Washington D.C. training sessions. With the defense attorneys, there was the usual showmanship, shouting, cajoling, and courtroom antics to arouse my anger. An angry witness is a poor witness, and in me the defense attorneys saw neither anger or fear. There was the usual verbal attack on my character, morals, marital status, education or lack of, and any innuendos regarding me being a traitor "to your people," as a liar, cheat, and so on. I had expected the onslaught, but not so severe. The prosecution objected but the court stated, "The agent seems to be able to handle himself," at which time I allowed myself the luxury of a smile, which infuriated the defense even more. After withstanding their barrages, I felt at the time that my testimony as to the facts in the case had not been shaken insofar as the jury was concerned. I could see this in the faces of the jury. Finally, cross-examination ended and re-direct testimony was held at a minimum by the government's co-prosecutor, Ron Goldfarb. Like Bill Lynch, Ron was a fascinating young attorney who led me through the testimony with ease. Many times since then I have said "Thanks Ron. There were many times at other trials that I wished for you and Bill. You guys really made me look good."

After my re-direct testimony I was excused by the court and permitted to remain in the courtroom for the remainder of the trial. I finally breathed a sigh of relief. It was over for me.

As the trial proceeded, I "rode shotgun" for one of the female employees of the Sportsman's Club, who had not testified as yet. She asked for protection each evening to her home and asked for me to protect her during the ride to and from her residence. A well-armed special agent drove the government car as she and I sat in the back seat. A photographer took our picture. I was well-armed as well. We both carried more firepower than our revolvers. The next day a photograph of us appeared in the local newspaper following our entering the vehicle and showed us cuddled as she sat close to me. Not funny at all to a married man. My fellow agents found it hilarious. Maybe that broke some of the tension that had built up during the lengthy trial. I still contend that she sat close to me not for any romantic notions, but for protection, because in those days, it would be unlikely that anyone would take a chance on a stray bullet intended for her to strike a federal agent.

Other agents testified regarding the raid, what was found and confiscated, and how the excise taxes were determined for criminal purposes. Eventually the trial ended and the jury found all eight defendants guilty as charged. It was rumored that Frank "Screw" Andrews had been so confident of acquittal that he had his golf clubs and luggage in his car trunk to leave immediately on vacation. The trial lasted a record twenty-three days. And so ended our involvement with Mr. Andrews.

A July 1962 issue of a local Cincinnati newspaper carried an article with photographs of six of the defendants:

> "Get Prison Terms
> (six photographs)1
> These six numbers racket figures, along with Frank "Screw" Andrews and _____, were sentence to five years in prison and fined $10,000 each in U.S. District Court, Covington, today on charges of conspiring to evade federal tax on gaming income."
>
> Another local newspaper carried the headline, *"Andrews Gets Five Years*—Numbers King Fined.$10,000; Co-Defendants Receive Prison Sentences"

All's well that ends well. We had broken the back of organized crime in Northern Kentucky. The people in Washington were ecstatic. Patterson and I hoped that this would be our last assignment in the Greater Cincinnati area. It was.

I returned to Youngstown (Bombsville-U.S.A.) Ohio, but there was still a long list of requests for the services of Owens and Patterson in some other part of the country. I suppose I considered this case the highlight of our career. In one case a District Court judge handed out a total of forty years in prison and $80,000 in fines in a single trial. Within a year I was promoted to the top grade for "bag-carrying" (field) agents.

Apparently Patterson and I did not go unnoticed by Internal Revenue officials in Washington, D.C. because early in 1963 I was asked to prepare a "white paper" (no pun intended) on undercover activity deficiencies, with no holds barred. I was instructed to bypass the regular chain of command and submit the paper directly to a specific person in their Washington office. I poured out my soul in that paper. I later learned that I was not the only special agent asked to prepare such a paper. I also learned that on the basis of those papers submitted to Washington, D.C., the person reviewing the documents concluded that a task force should be formed in Washington to pursue the matter further. Thus was born the Undercover School concept and the centralization of all major undercover activity within the Service.

Chapter Twelve

It was early in 1963, and I received another undercover assigned in the Galveston County, Texas area. My assignment was to place wagers in a numbers lottery and make such observations as necessary to obtain probable cause for arrest warrants. This was old hat. No problem.

When I arrived at a motel driving a bright red convertible Cadillac, bearing an Ohio license with letters and digits, I, with all the appearances of wealth, and driving a "hog," suddenly became the topic of discussion among the waiters, maids, and others at the motel and nearby taverns. I pounced upon my sudden popularity and suggested that I might have brought good luck with digits on my license plates, if people in Texas play the numbers. "Do we play the numbers? Boy, don't you know nothing?" After describing the numbers lottery, and how it was played, there were volunteers to take me to some action after they completed their shift at the motel/restaurant. They would consider it a favor if I let them take me to the numbers lottery location. I readily agreed and suggested that they "jump on it." That was my way of saying that my license plate numbers were hot. We left Houston proper and visited a picnic-looking area out in the country, with long lines of persons placing bets with someone at the head of each table. I was told that they had "drawings" several times during the day and evenings. When we reached the head of our line, the first thing I noticed was that sitting behind each table accepting the money and bets were white males. Even more noticeable was what some people would refer to as guns, but I would categorize the weapons as cannon without wheels. Also on the tables were huge stacks of currency, betting slips, and other gambling paraphernalia. I also noticed marked law enforcement vehicles in the area. With those loaded cannons on each table, why the police cars? There was no danger of anyone attempting to commit a robbery. Those law enforcement vehicles were there for another purpose. They escorted the lottery operators and their loot from the area to their homes or elsewhere. I placed bets on my favorite numbers but did not bet on my license plate for fear of bringing bad luck to my newfound friends.

I lost the battle but won the war. My favorite numbers did not hit, but like a storybook finish, the license plate numbers fell like clockwork. My co-workers have always contended that this was one of those fish stories told around camp fires. I had, in that short time, more than enough for a search warrant. I remained in the area and gathered more of the same until my assignment came to a sudden end. I signed an Affidavit for Probable Cause and immediately departed for Washington, D.C. as directed by an urgent request. As a result I did not participate in the raid, but later received newspaper accounts of what transpired. A local paper carried the following headline;

"Federal Agents Raid Galveston County, Nab 12."

Another local newspaper carried this headline:
"Texas City, Galveston Hit By Raids. Local Authorities Ignored as Feds Nab Policy Figures. What was described as one of the biggest policy rings operating in this part of the country was smashed Monday night when squads of Treasury Agents staged a series of six simultaneous lightning raids in Dickinson and Texas City."

Again, I remember something about that assignment that ordinarily would have been long-forgotten. On one of those occasions that I was in Galveston or nearby, I visited a seafood restaurant that I talked about for many years thereafter. Being a seafood lover, I scanned the menu, as the saying goes, "like a one-eyed cat peeping into a seafood store." I settled on a seafood platter that brought a quizzical look from the waitress. I asked if there was a problem to which she said, "No, but you are alone and really want a seafood platter?" I responded, "yes," to which she sighed and advised me to have a couple of drinks because it would take a while to prepare. After several drinks that were welcome in that 90 plus degree weather, I observed the waitress returning with what seemed to me to be a round dining room table without legs resting on her arm and shoulder. The platter was piled high enough with all of my favorites and other fish that I had never seen. I inquired as to whether that was all mine, to which she responded, "That's why I asked you if you really wanted a seafood platter." I knew that I could only eat a small portion of it and a doggy bag was out of the question in that heat. I took a relatively small portion of the platter, probably enough to feed two or three hungry people. I asked the waitress if she knew any families that would like a seafood dinner that night and if she could get the remaining feast to them. She seemed surprised, but stated that she knew many families that needed a meal every evening. I finished as much of my plate as I could and gave the waitress a generous tip. She thanked me profusely through watery eyes as I departed. When I waved good-by, and as I drove away, she was tearfully standing in the restaurant doorway.

I never had an opportunity to return, because of my sudden departure from that area, but whenever I visit a so-called fancy seafood restaurant I think of Galveston and my seafood platter. The closest I have come to that type of feast was when living in Washington, D.C. Down on the waterfront, I purchased various types of seafood from the boats at dockside on the Potomac and had a fish fry at our home for friends and relatives who visited.

My departure from Texas was very sudden. At the time I had no idea as to why I was recalled. Could it be because of my unorthodox methods in the field or had my identity been compromised? Whatever the reason, I was delighted to leave, inasmuch as scuttlebutt had it that local authorities could be hazardous to your health.

As I drove cross-country heading toward Washington, I thought that some of my deeds (or misdeeds) had finally caught up with me, because many of my methods of operation were not always according to the book. Actually, there was no book. I knew that I could not drive straight through to Washington from Texas, so I stopped in my hometown en route and was fortunate in getting my brother Albert to assist me in driving the remainder of the journey. We arrived in Washington in the early evening in my undercover fishtail, scarlet red, convertible Cadillac, commonly referred to on the street as a Hog. The evening of our arrival in Washington could have been the beginning of a long-range, deep penetration undercover project. In my trunk I always carried some of the tools of my trade in the form of two chess sets, two professional cameras, and a tape recorder with jazz and rhythm and blues tapes and albums. Who would ever believe me to be "the man." In any event, the evening was a success insofar as obtaining raw intelligence was concerned. I subsequently submitted a memorandum of my activities of that evening which included fraternizing with a major policy wheel operator and some of his underlings. We discussed the different types of numbers operations in various parts of the country.

Also, the plush establishment we visited was a gathering place for others in less-than-legal activities such as "fencing" stolen merchandise. However, my primary purpose for being in Washington was, as yet, unknown.

I arrived at the IRS National Office at the appointed time and was advised that the meeting would commence shortly. Also waiting in the room was a short, small, dapper young man, who greeted me with a casual smile, but no introduction. I greeted him similarly.

As to why we were called to Washington, I had no idea. Having served more than eight years in constant undercover situations, in most of the major cities, I again wondered whether some of my more unorthodox and sometimes bazaar actions in the field had finally caught up with me. I need not have worried. I was given a document to read prepared by Investigator Dante J. Bonomi, Alcohol, Tobacco, and Firearms Division, Internal Revenue Service, which was another "white paper" on current undercover techniques and their shortcomings. That person was not particularly protective of his career, but then, neither was I. I had had a strange feeling that the immaculately dressed young man across from me was the author of the document I was reading. I smiled inwardly as I recalled that my own paper could also be classified as a hot paper, inasmuch as it was unwise to verbally criticize top management in the National Office, and career suicide to do so in writing.

Our wait for the meeting to commence was not long as the dapper young man and I were summoned to a conference room where several persons were already seated. Formal introductions were made and the person I previously described was Alcohol, Tobacco and Firearms Investigator Bonomi. We were advised that the National Office was concerned about the failure of most of the agents attempting to work undercover and this initial session was to "pick our brains," review and discuss the papers we had previously submitted, and to organize an agenda with realistic timetables to implement a national program. Within a week we had established an agenda, timetable and tentative future meetings. Bonomi and I returned to our respective posts of duty and resumed our regular work. I assumed that like most meetings in Washington, nothing would come of it. Wrong again.

Not long thereafter I was again summoned to the National Office and learned that Bonomi and I had been assigned the task of preparing an undercover operations how-to manual or handbook. As I look back on that project, I realize that there were power plays and internal policies such as only Washington is capable of, but in our planned ignorance we were not deterred. It is my guess that in our ignorance we rode roughshod over the opposition and produced a document in record time. In those days, because of the countless levels of review, even a short one-paragraph memorandum was sometimes in the pipeline for weeks. We ignored chains of command and dealt with those who could be of assistance.

The premise on which our document was based involved several assumptions that have held true since the recording of history; those things that have gotten men, women, and even governments in trouble; the Three B's, but not necessarily in the order presented:

1. Booze (liquor)
2. Broads (women)
3. Bread (money)

Prior to assembling material for our manual, we contacted other federal law enforcement agencies to review their material relating to undercover operations in training their operatives. To our surprise and astonishment, no documents or formal training programs existed, or at least that was what we were told. We were on our own.

We were amazed that our original manuscript was accepted by those in need-to-know positions. It should be pointed out that Special Agent Norman Mueller of the National Office should be given credit for putting the document together in such form that it was acceptable even to those "in the ivory towers." There were many. Inasmuch as the prime motive for all illegal activity is money and power, there are no arguments that the Internal Revenue Service is in the unique position, with its statutory authority, to delve into the most secretive of transactions by any person. In my view, and that of many others, the Service was, and still is, in a position to fight organized crime and white-collar crime better than any other agency. As I previously pointed out, a case in point was Al Capone's conviction of tax evasion and sentenced to jail for 11 years. There are many who still believe that Eliot Ness and his Untouchables caused Capone's downfall. After our manual was approved, it was decided that Bonomi and I would establish a formal training program in Washington or elsewhere to train prospective undercover agents. The subject matter to be taught and dramatized would come right out of the handbook, but with special emphasis on the aforementioned Three

B's. The training program also emphasized believable cover stories, and completely backstopping such stories with high-quality documentation of the agents' backgrounds.

Unfortunately, though not unexpected, and over our strenuous objections, the first class was held in the basement of the National Office, with several academics from the Training Division as our advisors. We were not naïve and were well-aware of the purpose of their presence, which was to keep certain officials fully informed of our activities, and in some cases for their own selfish purposes, to become part of a cloak-and-dagger operation that was gaining some respectability in the Service.

The selection of candidates to attend the undercover school changed over the years, but the final selection of persons to attend the school rested with Bonomi and me. That never changed. In that connection, on more than one occasion we were referred to as real SOBs. We lost no sleep over the name-calling. We had been called much worse.

Lest I give the impression that the first school conducted in the basement of the IRS building was entirely in a formal classroom setting, I should point out that we spent much of the time in real-life situations in the field, much to the consternation of our Training Division advisors.

The typical special agents lifestyle, education, background, friends and relatives, was not conducive to the agent being literally thrown into the jungle of underworld characters such as gamblers, prostitutes, drugs and all the riffraff one encounters on the street. Bonomi and I considered that any successes we had would be measured by our ability to turn those lambs into wolves outwardly, before their training was complete. At the same time we had to make certain that their integrity was still intact and that they would not succumb to the temptations they would daily encounter. Many of the students survived the training, but many lacked the self-control, motivation or tenacity to survive out there in the hard, cruel world. Bonomi and I recommended that those agents should not be used in deep-cover situations. If we were overruled at the district office level, they invariably regretted not following our advice. The agents' downfall was usually one of the Three B's.

Our requests to conduct the undercover training outside of Washington, D.C. finally prevailed and schools were conducted elsewhere for many years. It would be inappropriate to discuss specific numbers, identities, successes or failures, but suffice it to say that there were a number of special agents with impressive records of undercover successes.

However, nothing taught at the undercover schools prepared the agents for what would be one of their most difficult problems to face: loneliness. One must play a make-believe role 24 hours per day, except in that lonely apartment or hotel room each night with no shoulder to cry on. There were so many of these nights for me I often wondered why I did not come in from the cold, and I certainly asked myself, "What am I doing here?" I never could answer those questions even for myself, and I certainly could not answer them for my wife and family. Bonomi and I have always ranked loneliness as the undercover agent's greatest enemy.

Sometime during the years we conducted the undercover schools, Bonomi transferred from the Alcohol, Tobacco and Firearms Division to the Intelligence Division and eventually headed the undercover group that operated out of the National Office. He can be credited with seeing that prior inequities in promotions, reassignments, travel funds, and complete backstopping of cover stories with adequate documentation was a thing of the past. Even more important, he constantly visited the agents in the field to assure them that they were not "out of sight, out of mind."

While the undercover schools were always conducted in an atmosphere of realism and seriousness, there were constantly humorous incidents that come to mind. One such incident, both serious and humorous at the same time, occurred on the evening of our first training session. The students were unobtrusively steered to a local Washington nightclub after a strenuous day, for a little R & R (rest and relaxation). The only advice given to them was to maintain their cover stories and undercover identities. They had been advised before they reported for the training to establish an undercover role and to maintain that role until advised otherwise by the instructors.

The following day the agents were asked to describe their prior evening at the club as to what problems, if any, they had encountered, such as their cover story not being adequate, or lack of answers regarding place of birth, school, employers, friends and associates. One would gather from the students' responses that they all had uneventful evenings.

At this point we played a tape recording of a conversation between a female and her male companion. The female sounded inquisitive and the male, who had more than enough to drink, seemed to tire of the questions and suggested that they retire to more intimate surroundings. The female advised that she had only met him that evening, knew nothing about him, and for all she knew he could be a gangster or some other dangerous character. The male voice stated that he was a special agent with the IRS Intelligence Division, attending a silly undercover school, and most of the other men in the club were also special agents using phony names. Now that she knew his true identity, there certainly was no reason that they should not follow through on his suggested "one night stand." Long before the tape ended one of the students had suffered the most embarrassing time of his life. There was more to come. At a signal from Bonomi and me, several females entered the classroom amidst groans coming from the class. Suddenly, one could hear a pin drop. The females were instantly recognized as the ones at the club during the prior evening. The class never learned how many of their intimate conversations had been recorded nor were they ever advised by Bonomi or me who had planted the girls in the club the previous evening. The students cried foul. We had dramatically proved our point. Enough said about two of the Three B's. This particular class was not unique and future classes were equally predictable in these make-believe situations which in the real world, could cost an agent his life or her life.

Another realistic incident that proved a point was in the handling of government funds by the students. At one of our schools each student was given a specific sum of money for use during our casino-type gambling training. The students were requested to keep detailed records regarding the funds provided and they would be required to settle up at the conclusion of that phase of their training. Some of the agents reported losses in specific amounts and dates, while other agents claimed losses but lacked specificity as to time and dates. Few returned their funds plus winnings. This episode led into our discussions regarding integrity and accounting for government funds. Bonomi and I were instrumental in accounting for confidential funds being incorporated in the Special Agents' handbook or manual.

Suffice it to say that those persons attending the undercover training departed a little less arrogant, but more self-assured and with a renewed set of standards. They were highly motivated and ready to take on the world, which many did.

African-American special agents figured prominently in the Service's undercover program over the years as can be attested to by the unit's chief, retired Supervisory Criminal Investigator Dan Bonomi. So many times the agents assignments took on roles never envisioned when the project started; incidents totally unrelated to the agents' reason for being in a particular location at a particular time. Special Agent Patterson and I were in Little

Rock, Arkansas during the school integration fiasco, which reminded us of an occupied city during World War II. We were stupid enough to remain in the streets and submit daily intelligence that had nothing to do with IRS matters. We received two bullet holes in our windshield as proof of our presence in Little Rock during the turmoil. To make matters worse, we had lodging accommodations at a house/hotel where the Afro-American newspaper people were housed. A curious photographer, who thought he recognized us as someone he knew, approached us on more than one occasion and stated, "It'll come to me. I know you guys. You're not reporters, and you're not Feds. The FBI don't have any of us." Patterson and I had immediately recognized the photographer as a reporter for the *Call &Post*, a weekly Cleveland African-American newspaper. Little Rock was not our target city., but a meeting place with our contact man, so we hastily returned to West Memphis, Arkansas and assumed our undercover roles.

Bonomi recalled one of the agents in his undercover group on assignment in California during one of those long hot summers, and rioters screaming "burn baby burn." This chaos had nothing to do with the agent's presence in that city, but the agent volunteered to remain and furnish daily intelligence regarding the rioters' plans and moves. Bonomi could cite numerous instances of the undercover agents being involved in situations that were not IRS related, but were useful to other law enforcement agencies.

I truly appreciate Mr. Bonomi agreeing to discuss, insofar as appropriate, his group's undercover operation. Because of my many years on the street, any attempt by me to relate the successes, failures, tragedies, and day-to-day frustrations would be less than objective.

This Is The Way It Was—by D. Bonomi

`I first came into government service as a Criminal Investigator with the A.T. & F. division and assigned to the Newark N.J. Area.

Within a short period of time, I was singled out for various undercover assignments. Most of the assignments were of the fringe variety and of limited duration. Since I was also conducting regular type investigations, I did not mind the undercover assignments.

In retrospect, early on I often felt that it may have resulted in a significantly different career direction if I had failed in one of the first undercover assignments.

This failure may have caused selection of others, which wasn't very difficult. During that time the agent was told what the assignment consisted of and where to start. One simply took off on the assignment with no backgrounding, documents or contacts. The agent hoped that he was glib enough and able to show the documentation that he had personally accumulated.

As a result of these assignments over the years I learned rapidly, accumulated documentation and a background and was then stereotyped and loaned out to other offices in need of undercover agents.

It has been well documented that with the appointment of Bobby Kennedy as Attorney General of the United States, we saw the real onset of a concerted federal effort to combat organized crime. One of the major deficiencies immediately apparent was the lack of intelligence and the ability to make inroads regarding organized crime groups. Within a short time, I was assigned to the Intelligence Division full time. In midsummer of 1963, I was officially transferred to the Intelligence Division.

One of the by-products of the Organized Crime Drive was the aforementioned meeting by a task force in Washington during the week of April 15, 1963. The objective of this task force was to review the shortcomings and faults of the undercover activities and establish a procedure by which a special group could be most efficiently trained, controlled and operated throughout the U. S.

`Needless to say, the prime mover of activities during these task force meetings was Hilton Owens. Those who know Owens are not surprised by that statement.

Notwithstanding the extensive experience gained by Owens up to that time, Hilton is a very bright, intelligent and articulate individual. It is also well known that he does not tolerate laziness and stupidly. He is and has been one of the most highly thought of and respected men in the Intelligence Division (African-American or White). One does not meet Hilton Owens, you experience him. If that sounds profound, then one should be exposed to his immediate family, along with his brothers. There is such a tremendous amount of intelligence, maturity and caring there that one is totally overwhelmed.

This April task force developed a total training program with a detailed curriculum, specific guidelines for central operations and control and for the first time, special and direct consideration for the undercover agent. A major reason for the success in compiling and implementing this program was due to the special efforts and support of the Assistant Director of the Intelligence Division, A. Robert Manzi.

The unit operated out of Washington, D.C., being administered by Special Agents in operations. In 1965, I (Bonomi) was transferred to the Operations Branch in Washington, D.C. and to the Unit as its Administrator.

If one recalls the climate that existed in the 1960s, vis a vis African-American/Whites, it is easy to understand the lack of objectives or assignments for African-American agents, which limited the number of African-American agents and sometimes dictated the type of assignments available to them. While not articulated very publicly or frequently, the African-American experiences encountered as special agents while undercover are totally unimaginable and frequently unbelievable. Being a supervising agent of a group that included African-American agents whom you introduced and injected into diverse situations, causes one to sit up and learn abruptly all of the nuances and innuendos. Can you imagine a white manager who is in dire need of a African-American undercover agent, will use him, but does not want to deal with him directly, because he is African-American?

Indirectly, the African-American agents could be thankful to Hilton Owens for the manner in which they eventually were accepted and treated, and for the more helpful and considerate attitude toward them in general and specifically for my outlook.

When the undercover training program was first started, Owens and I were called into Washington for three to four weeks. At the outset (first 3 schools) all of the agents were housed in hotels in downtown Washington, D.C. We always stayed at the Holiday Inn near Catholic University. Aside from the few times during that four weeks that we may have visited some local friends, Owens and I spent all of our time discussing the school and our personal as well as our professional experiences. Two people spending sixteen to eighteen hours a day for four weeks discussing and evaluating life styles will leave a strong impression on both. Most certainly, Owens' experience and exposure to many people with whom he worked also made it easier for the younger African-American agents.

Since the agents in the group were hand pick, supervision by me was not much of a problem. Infrequently, there were times when a problem may have been encountered due to a African-America agent having an unusual contact man who was white, and not too bright. By and large, the African-American agents were intelligent, articulate, enthusiastic and resilient. Since all of the agents were college graduates, the significant difference between the African-American and white agents was mostly social.

An additional advantage was an important consideration to me, the supervising agent. I not only instructed and made observations and evaluations at the school, I had the option of selecting what I considered the cream of the cream. It also appeared that one of the greatest additives was the philosophical approach to preparing the student for problems that he may encounter while on assignments. The objective was to describe to him and have him participate in a number of solutions to one problem, i.e., the problems encountered in the field are not always the way they were described and remedied at school. The agent learned when we presented or put him into a potential problem that he would also be given a number of actual solutions that were used by agents in the past.

As time went by, there also came about some dramatic changes in organized criminal activities that resulted in some new approaches and needs for African-American agents. In the early 1970s Columbians, Puerto Ricans, African-Americans and Cubans began "muscling in" on the known organized families and taking over the narcotics and gambling concessions usually controlled by the Cosa Nostra. At the time Hilton and I left government, these situations were coming to light very slowly, but at the same time, there began the unusual infighting by various federal agencies as to who was to control what and who was to become all-powerful again. Although there was a serious and rabid dislike and fear of undercover agents and operations, it seemed that somehow and somewhere undercover operations appeared to be the best way to uncover serious, large-scale crimes by the once untouchable criminals.

Perhaps the greatest milestone came about during the last two years of the group, before it was radically destroyed and plundered as though it were a living being for some Internal Auditors, who did not know what life existed after 5:00 p.m. The Intelligence Division, at that time, began hiring young people who had an interest in the division and had only one or two years of college. The position was similar to interning; the hire was assigned to a special agent or others in a group and developed experience while completing college.

Fortuitously, the unit had access to a young African-American man from Cleveland, Ohio, who was in his last year of college. The young man agreed to come to Washington and apply. Five minutes after the young man had been in my office discussing his background and the job, the impact he made was astounding. A very handsome young fellow, well dressed, neat, composed, articulate, well-spoken and low key. (Just like his mother Bea). As you would expect, we hired him. He stayed with the undercover group unit for a short while after completing college requirements to graduate. He has since become a special agent in Intelligence. The reason I look upon this situation as a milestone, is because I recall that the greatest impact on the start of the special group was Hilton Owens. When I left the group at retirement one of those I left administering was the young African-American agent from Cleveland, Ohio, Jerome Owens; the son of Hilton Owens (from everywhere).

Bonomi went on to state that discussing the curriculum at the Undercover School in detail would be inappropriate in this forum. Suffice to say that it was comprehensive, very realistic and demanding. Succinctly, always with class participation, we planned cover stories and documentation; dealing with the contact man; approaching and operating in the target area; pitfalls or problems; temporary or permanent withdrawal from the project; daily memorandums of activities and their content; practical problems; and a review of the rules of evidence, including entrapment; and finally, a checklist to ensure the undercover agent arrived at his destination without lacking basic needs for the project. The undercover operation was a success. However, there were persons in their ivory towers, who truly believed that heretofore untried techniques would cause nothing but trouble. To those persons, the fact that many undercover operations were successful was immaterial.

Even to this date, some of the undercover agents get together, embellish on the tall tales of their escapades and conquests, and I'm sure, silently wonder how or whether they could now survive in this violent, drug-ridden, crazy world.

Chapter Thirteen

Up to my Texas assignment, except on rare occasions, Patterson and I had worked as a team. However, because of numerous requests for our services, it was decided (not by us) that we should be separated and thereby reduce the backlog. Hindsight is always right, but everyone later agreed that this decision to separate us was a tragic mistake.

In November 1963 while I was in deep cover in Detroit, Michigan, I was contacted and advised that Special Agent Patterson was in critical condition in a Huntington, West Virginia, hospital from injuries sustained in a mysterious mountainside automobile crash. I picked up my wife in Cleveland and drove to the hospital where his wife was already waiting with several of our superiors from the Cincinnati Regional (now Central Region) office. We conferred with the attending physician and I was privately advised that Patterson would not survive the night. That comment to me from the doctor probably was for me to prepare his wife for the worst. I had no one to prepare me. We were permitted to see him. He was paralyzed from the neck down, and had suffered, among other things, a crushed chest and a severed spinal cord. I was also permitted to stay with him privately for a short time. We were told to return to our hotel and we would be advised if there was any change. It appeared that the doctor looked straight at me and I had to turn away. We returned to the hotel, but our wait was not long. He did not survive the night. That was best because he would have been a vegetable for the rest of his life. I was devastated, but I did not realize how much. Time is supposed to be the ultimate healer. It is not.

There was much speculation as to the specific cause and circumstances involved in the mysterious crash. I later met with our confidential informant who had been with Patterson shortly before the accident. No useful purpose would be served by relating our conversation or rehashing bygone days. Suffice it to say that I lost a partner and close friend, and insofar as my career was concerned, nothing would ever be the same. The only thing I could think of that night was that we were so young and now he was dead, because we were African-Americans and we had been used. I was angry at the time but that anger and frustration dissipated fairly rapidly because I knew that death can come while walking across the street or falling out of an amusement park roller coaster. However, I made myself a pledge that I would never accept another undercover partner, and I would retire the first day I became eligible. I kept both pledges. I continued to work undercover in Detroit as "Cadillac Ray, who lived in the glass house." I spent the better part of two years on that particular assignment. I was referred to as "Cadillac Ray" because I always drove a government-seized Cadillac convertible, and lived at the luxurious Lafayette Plaisiance apartment complex in downtown Detroit for much of 1963 and 1964. My favorite hangout was a tavern on John R Street. It was also a favorite location of numbers people, jeweled and expensively dressed patrons, police officers, and some just plain "good people," like the barmaid, and a cook with the southern touch. My frequent workouts at the YMCA's downtown Businessman's Club, which included jogging up to Belle Isle, kept me down to my fighting weight, because I seldom pushed away from the dinner table.

One Saturday afternoon while visiting my favorite tavern, several persons entered and also sat at the bar. I almost fainted, when one of them smiled and said, "Hi Flash, what the hell are you doing in Detroit?" The barmaid looked at us and asked the stranger, "Where do know him from?" "Flash and I ran on the same track team at Central High school in Cleveland back in . . .," he responded. "It was '40, '41 and '42, I responded. The visitor never mentioned me by name, only "Flash," as I was called by everyone on the school track team. His comments about me and Cleveland corroborated my cover story about my hometown. I remained at the tavern until he departed to be certain that he did not suddenly refer to me as Hilton Owens. He did not. I was safe at least for the time being. My next visit to the tavern was uneventful. No suspicious stares. Nothing out of the ordinary. That was only the first of two very close encounters with former acquaintances.

On another occasion, I was invited to a social function involving some of Detroit's elite. As my group approached several couples I almost had my second Detroit heart attack. I had known one of the couples for many years. The lady and her husband had visited her brother, who lived directly across the street from me on Cleveland's west side. This couple, as if forewarned, walked past me without the slightest indication that they recognized me. I never saw them again in Detroit during my stay there, but whenever we got together in Cleveland, they'd ask, "How'd we do?" I responded: "just great— our bumping into each other that night could have terminated my work in Detroit that night if you had introduced me as Hilton Owens from Cleveland."

I had no further calls in Detroit. Eventually, in 1964, I came in from cold, reporting back to my home district. However, without Patterson, my period of adjustment was difficult. Nightmares persisted and awakening in the middle of the night in a cold sweat was commonplace. Patterson's wife has remained one of our closest friends these many years. As a matter of fact, during a recent visit to our home, she observed me working on the manuscript for this book and considered it a worthwhile endeavor to enlighten the public of the price that some had to pay.

Chapter Fourteen

Throughout our careers together, Patterson and I were in different groups in the Cleveland office, but he did not enjoy a successful career insofar as regular criminal income tax prosecutions were concerned. As a result, his promotions suffered to the extent that I asked our National Office in Washington to intercede on his behalf, in getting him promoted. Prior to the latter office's intervention, I was two grades higher than Patterson and felt uncomfortable. I constantly argued with Cleveland District management that Patterson was not responsible for being constantly on the road and not able to successfully complete criminal cases. The district in turn, pointed to my record and stated, "But you managed to establish an impressive prosecution record." They were comparing me and Patterson, which was like comparing apples and oranges, an inappropriate, because other agents in the district were being promoted, whose prosecution records were similar to that of Patterson. The treatment of Patterson was one of the few gripes I had with the Service during my career, and that gripe was not with our division chief, Eldon R. Myers. As the saying goes, "He was caught between a rock and a hard place," in trying to do what was best for the division even if a particular individual might be hurt in the process. The system was screwed up.

However, Patterson's treatment, which I brought to the attention of officials in the National Office, and the treatment of others, as undercover activities accelerated, gave rise to the centralized undercover unit concept that is described elsewhere in this document.

Chapter Fifteen

I finally returned to my post of duty in 1964 after having spent most of 1955 through 1964 on the road.

Cleveland was my hometown as well as my post of duty and Cleveland, like most other major cities, was undergoing unrest and change. I was to become involved in that change.

My hometown is referred to as "The Best Location in the Nation," and on other occasions, "The Mistake on the Lake." We Clevelanders prefer the former description. I have lived many places, but Cleveland, Ohio will always be home.

It is not common knowledge but the legendary Eliot Ness served a tour of duty in Cleveland as safety director after his successes in Chicago. He later ran unsuccessfully for the office of Mayor in the late 1940s.

Like many major cities, Cleveland had its subcultures, gangsters, racketeers and poverty. During prohibition, with Cleveland being on Lake Erie, it was ideally located for bringing in liquor from Canada. The city and suburbia were also famous for lush gambling joints for the affluent, such as the Harvard Club and the Pettibone Club. As safety director, Eliot Ness was not as successful in Cleveland as he had been in Chicago. For the less affluent, there were the ever present after-hour joints and popular illegal numbers lotteries.

Cleveland's numbers lotteries were referred to as Clearing House and Policy. The clearing house name came from the stock market figures that appeared in the daily newspapers. Policy was also a form of lottery wherein a specific number of balls were placed in a bag, shaken thoroughly, and a drawing was held to determine the winning numbers. Crude portable printing presses printed the winning numbers immediately, so the writers could distribute the drawing slips immediately throughout the city. Folklore had it that this type of numbers operation derived its name "policy" because insurance collectors (debit men) visited industrial insurance policy holders each week and collected the nickels and dimes that paid the premiums. Many times the policy money was used to play the numbers and not pay the insurance premiums. Hence, the name policy was adopted to refer to the lottery.

As a small child in the early 1930s I recall being able to place a penny bet on numbers (policy) at White Fronts, which was a combination meat market and numbers drop. Even at that tender age, I knew that the steady stream of African-American males and females entering the establishment with brown paper bags were numbers writers. However, I had difficulty understanding why plainclothes and uniform police officers regularly visited the establishment and the writers and others in the establishment were not concerned; when on other occasions everyone scattered when the establishment was raided by the "flying squads." Life was complicated to a little child.

The passing years did not change that scenario to any great extent. The numbers racket flourished. The earlier years bring to mind Benny Mason, referred to by some as "the dean of the numbers racket." Even in the 1920s and 1930s, here was a African-American man that reportedly was netting more than a million dollars a year. He actually fed many of the poor in his "open kitchens" during the Depression. Many high school graduates, including myself, visited Benny Mason's farm on the outskirts of Cleveland on high school prom night. As I recall that was the occasion when many of us had our first drinks and could dance the night away. He undoubtedly subsidized those events, because we certainly exhausted our funds long before the evening ended.

I am not sure when he retired from the rackets. Ironically, in 1954, at age 60, he was killed in an automobile crash near London, Ohio. The funeral procession had almost 200 cars, and almost 500 persons attended the funeral. The minister summed it up.

> "Did he wait too late to make his peace with the Lord? I don't know— I'm trying not to get Benny Mason in heaven; that's up to someone else."
>
> "Benny's book is finished—let us hope that he and the Lord are on speaking terms."

Other numbers operators followed Benny Mason, but not in such a grand and unselfish style. I have no doubt that if Patterson and I had been around as special agents in his heyday, he would have been a prime target. His good deeds would not have mattered if the wagering tax laws had been in effect at the time, or that he helped the poor instead of paying his taxes.

As revenue officers and agents Patterson and I had no special concern about the illegal gambling. However, when we became special agents it then became our concern that the gambling fraternity was not purchasing wagering tax stamps and paying the 10 percent tax on bets accepted. We had frequently discussed doing for Cleveland what we had accomplished in Newport, Kentucky. We knew that we would eventually come in from the cold, and hoped to take on the task that few thought had any chance of success. They had thought the same thing of Newport, Kentucky. With Patterson's sudden demise, our chance never came. However, our district at least made a feeble attempt to enforce the wagering tax laws. But like the military picking civilian cooks to be truck drivers, the IRS could sometimes be accused of the same bureaucratic wisdom. The wrong people in the wrong slots. Even so, a plan was formulated and discussed with officials in Washington, who held the purse strings for such activities. There was general agreement that because the various numbers operations were in Cleveland's predominantly African-American neighborhoods, they would require experienced African-American undercover agents to infiltrate the organizations. We obtained the undercover agents we needed, all of whom I knew. I met with each of them as they arrived and reminded them of what Bonomi and I had emphasized at the undercover schools, i.e., "don't get stinking drunk; don't 'knock up' any of Cleveland's fair maidens, or fall head over heels in love; don't misuse the government's money, and don't fraternize with each other." I could have saved my breath, because each of them was an old hand at working undercover, and listened, but did not necessarily heed my preaching. Fortunately, only two of them fell in love, but no children ensued. None needed to be bailed out of jail for drunk driving, nor did they throw government money around like drunken sailors on leave. I knew most of the regulars at the night clubs, restaurants, and other establishments, and frequently visited the establishments. My visits did not create any undue alarm because in earlier years Patterson and I had made it a practice to "make the rounds," corroborating information received from our network of informants. We had a lot of IOUs out there in the ghetto.

During the time we had the substantial number of undercover agents operating in the city's ghettos, I did not receive any feedback from informants that the city was hot. However, several informants mentioned that the police were becoming a little more active, but no big thing. I did not agree with my superiors' determination to use our local agents simultaneously, in attempting to conduct surveillance of the numbers operators and their writers/pickup men (and women), in the city's African-American communities. Fortunately, the surveillance teams did not cause any great damage. The undercover agents advised me that when the surveillance teams were spotted by the writers and pickup men, they were thought to be locals with their usual harassment. I closely guarded the intelligence gathered by the undercover agents so that the surveillance teams would not be furnished with specific information on which they might prematurely act.

The undercover agents' activities sometimes carried them beyond the gambling fraternity. Suffice it to say that they were successful in infiltrating closed professional and social groups, political circles, sports enthusiasts, and a variety of other endeavors. Not knowing how much manpower and time could be devoted to this project, I reminded the agents to concentrate on the matters at hand, i.e., gambling.

The numbers game, and Alex "Shondor" Birns, were our primary targets. Birns was always in the background, while his cronies, the visible African-American operators, flashed their fancy cars, women, clothes, and money.

Birns had been a thorn in the side of law enforcement for most of his adult life. He was born in Austria-Hungary (now Czechoslovakia) in 1905. His family brought him to the United States about a year later. He grew up on Cleveland's east side, which later became part of Cleveland's ghetto. He is reported to have been an excellent athlete in secondary schools. He had more than 50 arrests, starting with auto theft in 1925. He had a rap sheet that anyone in the underworld would be proud to own. He was never naturalized, but efforts to deport him were unsuccessful. He was classified as a criminal alien. During World War II, he was ordered interned in January 1943 for the duration of the war, but released in June 1944. He was convicted in 1954 for income tax evasion and served three years in a federal penitentiary. In 1967 he was convicted of perjury for lying to IRS regarding his assets, and was again sentenced to three years in a federal penitentiary. He had numerous arrests involving assault, battery, and other crimes. Apparently he learned his lesson regarding his wealth after his 1954 bout with the IRS, because in later years, a business associate stated that when Birns needed money he merely went into the coffee can buried in backyard. Law enforcement officers looked for that coffee can. He was once labeled "Cleveland's Public Enemy No. 1."

In 1975 his luck took a turn for the worst. The *Cleveland Call & Post,* a African-American weekly newspaper, carried the following story:

> The March 29 bombing death of Cleveland numbers racketeer Alex (Shondor Birns has prompted speculation that African-American racket figures had the job done and are preparing for an all-out gang war to gain entire control of the multi-million dollar policy and numbers operations controlled by the 70-year old kingpin.

He was killed when his 1975 Lincoln Continental Mark IV was bombed. According to newspaper accounts, his funeral was attended by well-dressed associates, Short Vincent cronies and lawyers. (Short Vincent referred to a street in downtown Cleveland where the well-heeled socialized). The illegally parked Cadillacs and Lincoln Continentals on Short Vincent were seldom found with parking tickets on their windshields, except occasionally just before election time. Although this was an area not frequented by African-Americans, one of our undercover agents developed a rapport with a frequenter of Short Vincent, but was not successful in getting close to Shondor Birns.

We were confident that with time, and our daily contacts with the gambling fraternity, we could build another income tax case, as well as wagering tax violations against Birns and his cohorts.

It became apparent to me that management would not permit this project to develop into a deep-penetration, long-range affair. They expected results in the short run. The undercover agents were in deep, but immediate results would come in the form of superficial raids on principals' homes, numbers drop locations, and probably some arrests of lower-echelon individuals. We had rumors and hearsay, but nothing solid on Shondor Birns that would hold up in court. The undercover agents had sufficient bets with writers of all the major operators, and other data necessary to raid the residences, numbers' locations, seize vehicles, and make arrests. Such raids received news coverage, but were not of much benefit in making successful felony income tax evasion cases.

It was decided that simultaneous raids should be conducted throughout the city. Special Agent Greg Michael, an attorney, was brought in from our Toledo office, to prepare the all-important Affidavits for Probable Cause for search and arrest warrants. The memoranda from each of the undercover agents was sorted, reviewed, and collated. I visited each of the locations where search warrants would be executed and obtained accurate descriptions of each location.

In the past there had been occasions when a place raided was next door to the actual location. Generally, the culprits watched with amusement as our agents broke down the wrong door, apologized to the tenant, and returned to the office.

In some instances, the bets made by the undercover agents were not properly described in the agents' daily memoranda and the agents were asked to go through the betting exercises several more times before the actual raids.

Generally, by the time the Intelligence Division was ready to conduct raids, we had sufficient evidence to indict and convict without the actual raid. However, the raids were frosting on the cake, resulting in much-needed news coverage for the Service, as well as arrests, seizure of currency, vehicles, gambling paraphernalia, and leads to those insulated from daily activities. It was our hope that the raids would lead to the target, Alex "Shondor" Birns.

Based on the detailed Affidavits for Probable Cause meticulously prepared by Special Agent Greg Michael, search warrants were easily obtained for a half-dozen locations. Arrest warrants were obtained for several (principals) operators and their writers.

Simultaneous raids were conducted at six sites, including residences, four record shops, and a tavern owned by one of the operators. Agents found betting slips and other gambling paraphernalia at some of the residences, including approximately $2,500 in currency and several hundred pounds of coins, all of which was seized. Agents found bet slips, gambling paraphernalia, and a record amount of currency at one of the residences. They found the wife in bed in the upstairs bedroom, recuperating from recent surgery. Also in the room they found huge quantities of currency in dresser drawers. After over five hours of counting by our special agents, the money totaled over $305,000. When the currency was discovered, the raid leader asked for additional help, and agents were diverted from other locations to assist in the counting and re-counting of the currency. The money was again counted and then taken to the Federal Reserve Bank in downtown Cleveland. While the raids were in progress, agents fanned out over the city in search of those persons for whom we had search warrants. The lottery operator's home where the huge cache of currency was found was among those arrested. He joked with the agents in his home while they slowly counted the currency, and demonstrated his finger dexterity, indicating that he could have counted the cache faster than the entire group of special agents.

When one of the operators learned that there was a warrant for his arrest, he and an associate surrendered to the United States Commissioner. His associate's wife had been arrested the previous day, along with a half dozen other writers. Each of the persons arrested was charged with accepting wagers without first obtaining a $50 wagering tax stamp, a federal misdemeanor.

For the better part of a week, Cleveland's east side gambling fraternity was shook up, wondering what other persons would be arrested. The undercover agents did not participate in the raids or the searches. I, as well as the police officers accompanying us, was acquainted with the persons sought, and there was no need to burn the undercover agents until absolutely necessary.

I think that a *Cleveland Call & Post* newspaper reporter summed it up beautifully. He wrote: (excerpted)

> *$305,000 CACHE FOUND BY T-MEN STUNS E. SIDE*
> Police raids, racketeers, big hits, hot numbers, so what? Cadillacs, chitterlings, and champagne and caviar, on the East Side, this is old hat, like bombings, shootings, you get those. But $300,000 in cash, say w ha-a-t? . . .
>
> That's how much "they" got from the house of Wilbur Dean at 10915 Wade Park Avenue.
>
> "Wait a minute—Wilbur Dean, who the hell is he—and did you say $300,000 in cash—you mean a Negro had all that money in his home.
>
> *Oh Yea*—only it was $305,000, right in his bedroom, and man, they say he *showed* it to 'em, when Internal Revenue agents and police raided the house with a search warrant Monday.
>
> *Showed* it to 'em—what do you mean—who's going to invite police to come upstairs and take a look at all that kind of money?"

Well, that's the story, and it was neatly tucked away—if all that money can be neat—in bundles—51 of 'em, of ten, twenties, with some fifty-dollar bills, it actually happened.

Wilbur Dean—Who is he? Oh, you know, the guy who operates those House of Jazz record shops, one at 1454 Addison Road—to remember, it was bombed little more than a year ago—and another at 8508 Hough Ave., and one at 1496 East 66th St., the police say.

You mean, he's in the numbers— yeah, but he is no big timer, is he? If he isn't, who IS?

"But I thought—how did they know to go there—why didn't they hit him before?

Well, this was a federal raid, y'understand the Internal Revenue Agents, but they had the Cleveland Police with 'em—you know, when Uncle Sam hits, he hits 'em, boy!

Yeah, Uncle Sam kept hitting 'em this week, all over the East Side in surprise raids with some arrests. They're after gamblers who didn't pay the Federal Tax Stamp of $50, you see.

Man, federal agents were as thick as flies, they were stomping up Cedar Ave, four abreast well, you know, you could see they weren't kidding now.

"Let's see, they picked up a lot of cars, new cars'n all, and a lot of well—known names . . . including Wilbur Dean, the guy who had the $300,000 stashed in his bedroom got $2,500 and a huge sack of coins at . . .

Yeah, Fine—but, how about that $305,000 in cash, what about that?

This seizure received widespread newspaper coverage. It was the largest seizure of currency in the country involving a numbers operation, on record, up to that time.

That was only the beginning. The seized $305,000 required more than fifteen special agents over five hours to count, tally, recheck and bundle the currency, which was in small denominations. It filled two post office mailbags.

The case went to U.S. District Court and a local Cleveland newspaper ran a March 12, 1966 article that stated: *"Deans Lose $305,626, Government Takes All"*

Excerpts from the newspaper article read:

> Uncle Sam held the high card in a winner-take-all case in the Federal Courtroom of U. S. Judge, Tuesday where the judge ruled _____ would not get one nickel of the $305,626 seized from the Dean home last year. The high-stakes curt battle, a civil case for the biggest cash prize in the annals of U. S. Courts, was waged for more than a week by Assistant U. S. Attorney James L. Oakar against two prominent Negro attorneys . . .

They filed a petition to appeal the decision of the District Court judge. The appeal was turned down by the U.S. Circuit of Appeals, 6th Circuit. Now retired Supervisory Criminal Investigator Greg Michael, then Special Agent Greg Michael, of our IRS Toledo office, can be given credit for organizing the raiding parties; preparing the Affidavits for Probable Cause for the search warrants; and testifying most impressively at the hearing in district court. The undercover agents were credited with making the raids possible and successful.

The Intelligence Division in Cleveland continued to make sporadic raids and arrests, but nothing compared to the Dean seizure. There were those that stated the Dean seizure was pure luck, but there's an old saying, "The harder you work, the luckier you get." Many of us worked hard, and some of us were sometimes lucky.

During those hectic years the then IRS Intelligence Division and a special investigation unit of the Cleveland Police Department under the command of Lt. Martin P. Cooney cooperated in many numbers lottery investigations. With Sergeants Dever, DeLau, and McCool, the experts in the numbers lottery field, patiently enlightening our staff, we developed the expertise necessary to make federal cases out of matters that would have been relegated to civil litigation. For this we were most grateful, particularly those agents that had not been exposed to Cleveland's underworld and innocence insofar as gambling was concerned. I recall that Sergeant Dever suddenly died in 1966 of a heart attack, probably never knowing how we felt about their unit. It's many years too late, but better late than never, so "thanks guys." I am sure if the late Special Agent Patterson were around, he'd thank you also.

It is ironic that numbers lotteries, illegal and the subject of many arrests and convictions, are now a national pastime and at this writing, a Pennsylvania jackpot exceeded $113 million. Twenty and $thirty million dollar jackpots are now commonplace. More than 30 years ago Patterson and I discussed the pros and cons of legalized gambling and were in complete agreement that in our lifetime we would see people placing bets on numbers in public places, but never in our wildest dreams did we visualize multimillion-dollar-type payoffs. We also believed at the time that Las Vegas-type casinos would spread beyond Nevada, and were also right in that regard. We were ahead of our time. Only time will tell whether the first five cities we guessed would have legalized casinos will prove correct.

Chapter Sixteen

I was subsequently promoted to Supervisory Criminal Investigator (group supervisor). My group encompassed Cleveland and Akron, Ohio posts of duty and consisted of approximately 10 special agents and support staff at each location. I alternated between the two offices every other day. Thus, I became the first African-American special agent to attain a supervisory position in the Intelligence Division nationwide. I did not experience any particular problems as a supervisor because I had worked alongside many of the agents in my group and they knew me as a no-nonsense, bottom-line type of individual. Suffice it to say that my group attained a highly successful prosecution record during my stay. We retired Cleveland District special agents are still a close-knit group getting together each summer and telling war stories that seem more elaborate each passing year.

In 1969, an unusual opportunity came to my attention. High-ranking government officials in Washington, D.C. decided to establish another Organized Crime Strike Force in Manhattan. Basically, the Strike Force concept was for all federal law enforcement agencies to combine in an all-out war on organized crime through a joint cooperative effort. I was selected to be one of the four Intelligence Division Representatives on what was officially known as the "Manhattan Joint Strike Force." It had not only federal law enforcement officers but state and local as well.

Our mission was to develop a comprehensive program to investigate all five organized crime families in the New York area. Even at this writing 20 years later, Strike Forces are still operating in many cities. However, in January 1990, after more than a year of controversy and bickering with Congress, Attorney General Dick Thornburgh imposed his long sought-after change. Strike Force attorneys are now under the control of local U.S. Attorneys. Thornburgh had been an opponent of the strike force concept ever since he was U.S. Attorney in Pittsburgh and the Strike Force attorneys in Pittsburgh were not accountable to him. At that time Strike Force attorneys reported directly to the Department of Justice in Washington, D.C.

Our assignment to the strike force was for a two-year period. In my particular case it covered mid-1969 through mid-1971, and we strike force representatives were proud of our accomplishments in developing an overall program for the Internal Revenue Service in the joint effort of waging an all out war on the five organized crime families in New York. However, the strike force concept called for a long range commitment and a continual infusing of resources from the various federal agencies.

In his 1988 Annual Report, the Commissioner of Internal Revenue alluded to Strike Forces, indicating the Service's continued support of the concept. He stated,

Organized Crime Task Forces

The IRS is strongly committed to working with other federal agencies in combating organized crime through participation in the various Department of Justice strike force programs. The strike force approach presents a coordinated pursuit by law enforcement agencies of organized crime members and their criminal activities.

Successful prosecutions weaken organized crime by breaking up its organization and by removing major crime figures from their positions in the criminal hierarchy.

The IRS believes that devoting substantial resources to the investigation of organized crime is appropriate not only because of the significant amount of unreported income but also to maintain public confidence that IRS administers the tax laws fairly and evenly.

In a recent case in Miami, a large tax shelter was uncovered. It was revealed that the tax shelter was bankrolled by a loan shark from Chicago organized crime family. When the mobster realized how profitable the scam was he extracted about two million dollars from the principals behind the operation. The various people involved in this scam received prison sentences totaling over sixty years.

After completion of my temporary Strike Force assignment I returned to my group supervisor position in Cleveland in1971 for approximately one year. I then transferred to the National Office, Washington, D.C. in 1972 and retired as a Supervisory Criminal Investigator (Area Manager) in January1975. At the time of my retirement I was the highest ranking African-American in the Intelligence Division in Washington, and the first African-American to serve a full twenty years in the Intelligence Division and retire.

Those twenty years (1955-1975) passed very fast. I certainly have forgotten more than I can remember of those years. We tend to forget the pain and unpleasantness with the passing of time. Unfortunately, researching and writing this manuscript brought back many of the memories, both the good and the bad, particularly with regards to my partner and friend, Curtis Patterson. Even with the diaries we were required to maintain, I probably could not recall a complete chronology of events. I suppose when one reads of the activities of Special Agent Hilton Owens they might ask, "What did he actually do for twenty years?" My answer would be: "It passed too fast to totally recall."

Post—Retirement

I suppose being the first African-American Supervisory Criminal Investigator to serve 20 full years in the division and retire would attract some attention, even in some foreign circles. I decided against any further cloak and dagger projects and therefore declined to discuss post-retirement employment involving any foreign intrigue.

I accepted a number of positions, such as a short stint as Chief, Bureau of Special Investigations, Department of Public Aid, State of Illinois. Welfare fraud was prevalent in the agency, with a $1.2 billion budget. Politics played a major role in the department and it was obvious to me from the outset that I was expected to fall in line. Too much interference for me. I resigned after several months on about a four hour notice.

One of my more interesting post-retirement positions took me to Jamaica, West Indies. The late G. Troy Register, Jr., retired Chief, Intelligence Division, Jacksonville District formed Professional Financial Services, Inc., Miami, Florida, which acquired a service contract with the Government of Jamaica. Also, John J. Olszewski, retired Director, Intelligence Division, Washington, D.C., was part of the organization. Our primary mission was to assist the Ministers of Finance and National Security in developing a formal program to train their personnel in preventing an outflow of wealth and improve their foreign exchange posture. In that connection we developed a how-to handbook similar to the special agents' handbook and part IX of the IRS manual. The document covered accounting, modern business concepts and investigative techniques. I was fortunate in eventually conducting many of the training sessions and became the resident advisor. The how-to document was titled "Financial Investigative Unit Manual," and was issued by the Minister of National Security. The document was tightly controlled and my copy was Number 007 –an omen. The introduction in the manual stated, "The mission of the Financial Investigative Unit is to further the total Government objective of encouraging and achieving the highest possible degree of voluntary compliance with the Exchange Control Act, Income

Tax Laws, Excise Tax Laws, and Trade Board Regulations or other Acts or Laws enacted to protect the revenues or other economic interests of the Government." The Financial Investigative Unit, commonly, but not affectionately known as the FIU, consisted of constabulary (police), Customs, Immigration, tax department agents, and personnel from other government agencies. It is a matter of public record that the FIU was highly successful in stemming the flow of currency out of Jamaica. Those two years were most rewarding to me personally in that I could see the immediate results of our formal training program, the use of the manual, and the tangible evidence of the FIU's success in unraveling the most devious attempts to circumvent the Exchange Control Act. Those types of cases received the widest news coverage and was the talk on the streets of Kingston and elsewhere in the island nation. Budgetary constraints caused our departure, but subsequent feedback to me from knowledgeable sources assured me that the FIU continued to enjoy extreme success.

This assignment lasted two wonderful years and I learned to eat salt fish (cod) as only the Jamaicans can prepare it, curried goat, boiled bananas, and drink overproof Appleton rum.

My Jamaican friends contend that I, a serious amateur photographer, probably possessed the most complete set of photographs on the island.

Returning to Jamaica someday is a must. I was affectionately referred to as the "Ja'merican." Another memorable post retirement position I held was with the Virgin Islands Bureau of Internal Revenue during four separate one-year tours of duty spanning fourteen years.

I first arrived on St. Thomas in 1979 and departed in disgust for the final time in the fall of 1993.

Shortly after I arrived I was told to read a book by Herman Wouk titled: "Don't Stop the Carnival." The "tongue in cheek" plot supposedly took place on a mythical island in the Caribbean. I immediately read the book and was in for a rude awakening. I was soon to learn that I was living and working on that mythical island.

In 1978, it had come to the attention of the Internal Revenue Service in Washington that I had served two years in the Caribbean with the Government of Jamaica, and I was asked by officials in Washington, D.C. if I would be interested in returning to the Caribbean. My immediate response was "Yes." I was advised that the Virgin Islands Bureau of Internal Revenue, known then as the Tax Division, was in need of someone with criminal tax investigative experience to establish a Criminal Investigation Division within their Bureau. I accepted the position. My primary mission was to establish a unit similar to that in the Service. I learned that the Internal Revenue Code was in effect in the Virgin Islands under what was termed the "mirror theory." For all practical purposes, the only difference in the Virgin Islands tax code was the substitution of the words "Virgin Islands" wherever in the U.S. code the words "United States" appeared. Under that theory, tax returns were processed in the same manner as in the Internal Revenue Service. Additional assessments were made by internal revenue agents in their Audit Enforcement Branch, and delinquent taxes were collected by their revenue officers just as on the mainland. Residents of the Virgin Islands are considered to have met their federal income tax obligations by filing a U.S. Individual Income Tax Return, Form 1040, with the Government of the Virgin Islands. The taxes collected remained in the Virgin Islands' Treasury.

However, they did not have a Criminal Investigation Division to investigate alleged criminal tax violations. My job was to establish such a division, which was not a difficult task. Many tactical problems were encountered, primarily because of budget constraints. I noted from the outset that the local internal revenue agents did not wish to become involved in a joint investigations of Virgin Islands' taxpayers.

However, a conscientious young revenue agent joined me in an investigation and conviction of a locally prominent attorney for alleged tax evasion.

That agent later became the Virgin Island government's inspector general. During that same year a cement contractor was convicted for willfully failing to truthfully account for and pay over taxes withheld from his employees' wages. Those cases received widespread coverage by the news media.

Because of the "Don't Stop the Carnival" conditions that existed at the time, such as no government vehicle, no secretary, and no office supplies, I declined to renew my contract. Working in the Virgin Islands, in addition to the high cost of living, I had to use my personal vehicle with no mileage reimbursement, type my correspondence and investigative reports, and purchase any needed supplies, all of which required a substantial outlay of my personal funds. It was not the fault of the director of the Bureau, but the legislators apparently did not see fit to do justice to the Bureau's requirements. The Senators apparently took the position, "Don't give them too much, they may harass my constituents, or even worse, me." After that first year I returned to my home stateside. Actually, those two criminal cases received substantial news media coverage, and the Chief of the Processing Branch advised me that there was a significant increase in the number of delinquent tax returns being filed.

Failure to file and tax evasion was rampant in the islands, and the conviction of the prominent attorney, which few expected would happen, caused considerable conversation on the street. I considered it prudent to carry my weapon at all times, which I did. I received no direct threats, but on one occasion the attorney before an audience, loudly threatened to throw my cooperating agent down steel stairs. I immediately interceded and advised the taxpayer that I would not hesitate to arrest him on the spot if he persisted, even in verbal threats, or attempted in any manner to carry out his threat. There was no need to make an arrest. When the taxpayer noted that I was armed and prepared to arrest him in front of his cronies, he retreated from his menacing stance. No arrest was necessary and the internal revenue agent and I departed. The investigation proceeded without any further disturbances.

About one year after my return to the mainland, I was again contacted by the director of the Bureau and asked if I would return. According to the director, all of the problems encountered during my first tour of duty were now resolved and I would receive a government vehicle, a secretary, office supplies and equipment. It was not difficult for him to convince me to return. I have always disliked leaving a job unfinished, and establishing a viable criminal tax program in the Virgin Islands was still my objective.

During my second tour of duty we were unable to obtain funds needed to hire local special agents, so I was again required to wear many hats, i.e., special agent, reviewer, special agent-in-charge, typist, and an expert witness at the trial. Further, funds promised to the director did not materialize. Even so, we were again successful in a highly publicized failure-to-file case involving a taxpayer who, with his brothers, owned valuable commercial real estate comprising downtown shops frequented by the tourists. I was advised that delinquent tax returns poured in, which we equated to the news coverage of the trial by jury and accompanying conviction. At the end of this second one-year contract I again declined to renew my contract and returned to the mainland.

I subsequently served two additional tours of duty with the Bureau of Internal Revenue. My last tour of duty, for all practical purposes, ended on February 8, 1993, when the director informed me in the presence of three of his senior staff members that he had unilaterally decided to terminate an active criminal investigation. His reasoning escapes me even now, but he mentioned that to continue the investigation would be embarrassing to the current administration and would cause discord in the inner circle. At that point I probably gave the director the worst tongue-lashing he had encountered since he was a small child. There are those who might say I threatened him with prosecution because I reminded him that CID had recommended prosecution against many high-ranking politicians and government officials, including a former Commissioner of Internal Revenue. I also advised him to furnish me a memorandum stating categorically that he had terminated a criminal investigation and set forth in specific terms the reason for the termination. No such memorandum was forthcoming. For a number of months following our confrontation he refused to confer with me regarding CID matters. As a matter of fact during a meeting of his senior staff members where I was absent he informed them that I would not be renewing my contract and he might have CID taken over by the Audit Branch. When I departed in the fall of 1993, my association with the Bureau had covered a span of 14 years. It is unfortunate that the size of the Bureau would preclude it from having an Inspection Service, because at a minimum I would have referred the matter to that office for possible charges of "unauthorized disclosure" of tax information and possible "obstruction of justice." As it now stands, he may "close down" the criminal investigation activity, or permit it to function, but he closely monitor who is investigated for tax violations. A simple solution but very controversial undertaking would be for IRS to step in and take over the criminal investigation program. Congress considered a proposal in the late 1970s to take over the tax administration in the Virgin Islands, but the Carter Administration "backed off" when prominent Virgin Islanders threatened to go to the United Nations and yell: "Back to colonialism."

It was time for me to say "enough." Anyone having read Herman Wouk's book about a mythical Caribbean Island titled "Don't Stop the Carnival" would understand why a "yankee" or "continental" as we are sometimes called would pack up and go home and return only for the sun, the sand, and the sea.

I told my former business associates, family, and friends that I had finally retired after about nineteen years in semi-retirement. My wife always rebuffed my retirement comments with a statement of her own, which is, "Just let someone make him an offer he can't refuse, we'll be gone again. I'm packed and ready."

PART II

William E. Mannie

Dedication

To Lucy Coleman, my wife's grandmother and my kid's great-grandmother, for being extremely helpful when our needs were so great.

A Special Thanks To

My wife Jessie, for being patient and understanding during my formative years as a special agent.

Self Portrait—Bill Mannie

Few of us take the time to look into the mirror and wonder whether who we saw is in the same perspective by others around us. Bill Mannie did just that and labored over the task for many years until he finally wrote an emotional dissertation on himself, which he had forgotten. I found it while rummaging through his personal papers. When I read it to him, if people of 'color' can blush, he did. Unabridged, his self-portrait follows:

If I am criticized, at least I believe that some of this criticism must be true. If I am praised I treat this as mere vanity. For my faults are numerous; yet controllable enough to make me an appreciable person; perhaps even to a fellowship person who shows signs of erratic kindness and consideration. I never, by design, hurt anyone; nor do I wish anyone sadness or ill will. I do not care to injure a person physically or mentally—furthermore, I consciously feel responsible for any and all inflictions I might cause another, regardless. Because of this trait, I am extremely careful of expressing my thoughts and feelings to others—I literally walk on eggs in feeling my way through a conversation with a person who I might have a few negative thoughts about him or her. I have a tendency to overemphasize the positive and de-emphasize the negative. This has always been my weakness; I will not, or have never permitted this trait to interfere with important and sensitive decisions. I usually delay the sad part of any conversation; yet I become extremely repetitive with "good news," so repetitive that I might, in some instances, become a negative myself or create a "wish you close syndrome."

This is the Bill Mannie you will be reading about.

Notice of Personnel Actions

Action	Effective Date	Grade Position
Appointment	July 7, 1958	GS-5 IRA
Promotion	January 11, 1959	GS-7 IRA
Reassignment	January 25, 1959	GS-7 SA

Promotion	March 6, 1960	GS-9 SA
Promotion	May 14, 1961	GS-11 SA
Promotion	February 3, 1963	GS-12 SA
Promotion	February 13, 1966	GS-13 SA
Reassignment	April 7, 1968	GS-13 Supr
Promotion	July 26, 1970	GS-14 Supr
Retirement	January 4, 1984	

Commendations and Awards

Superior Performance Award with Outstanding Rating—1964
Recommended for the Federal Employee of the Year Award—1965
Finalist, Federal Employee of the Year Award—1967
Letters of Commendation from the United States Attorney Letter of Commendation from E. P. Trainer, Regional Commissioner—1972
Superior Quality Step Increase Award—1972
Sustained Superior Performance Award—1973
Sustained Superior Performance Award—1974
District Group Managers' Award—1882

Chapter Seventeen

Introduction

Bill Mannie was born on January 19, 1931 in Helena, Arkansas, one of four children. He could recall their grandparents' place, called the "big house." He and his family lived in a small house also on the grandparents' property. He recalled his father's death in 1936. He also recalled the one-room segregated schoolhouse in their farm area and the "jelly bucket" lunch pails. After his father's death, his mother moved to Chicago and the children moved to Helena, living with an aunt, where they attended school in the city proper. Later, an aunt took them to Chicago to be with their mother. That was in 1937. Because of the notion that southern schools were inferior, Chicago school officials put him back a full year. Later in high school, Bill attended makeup classes and graduated at eighteen, although he normally would have graduated at seventeen. He was reared, educated and married in Chicago where he has remained, except for a four-year stint in the U.S. Air Force.

His childhood buddy, later to be his wife, and he, from about age twelve, had frequently talked about getting married on a Saturday, Valentine's Day. While on leave from the Air Force in 1953, they fulfilled that dream and were married on Valentine's Day. During the ensuing years they had four children, including twins. Their two sons are college graduates and certified public accountants; their eldest daughter attended college and entered the high-tech industry in its infancy and progressed both financially and otherwise just as her brothers. The youngest daughter, still in school, has also entered the computer field, but her primary goal is obtaining that piece of paper, her degree.

After graduating from Wendell Phillips High School In 1949, Bill enrolled in Wilson Junior College (now Kennedy King Junior College) on Chicago's south side, with a pre-med/zoology major, and subsequently received an associate's degree. He then entered the University of Illinois on a similar course, but because of an overlapping of courses already taken, he decided to enroll in Roosevelt University, another four-year institution. The Korean War was in full swing. Bill received a draft notice and he recalled, "I panicked, and enlisted in the Air Force for four years." He left Chicago in March 1952, 21 years old and engaged, and was shipped to an Air Force base in San Antonio, Texas.

It was suggested to Bill by Air Force personnel that he apply for pilot training, in which he was not interested. He stated, "Those guys went over and did not come back." He took a number of examinations related to flight training and passed all tests, except one which related to his equilibrium. He could not recall whether he consciously failed. He was assigned to the Medical Corps, and recalled "silently screaming with joy," because his first love was medicine. After further training he served his remaining three-and-one-half years as a surgical nurse, a job for which he had been trained and which he thoroughly enjoyed.

As fate will sometimes intervene, Bill met a patient at the hospital who was a reserve officer and seemed familiar with the Federal Bureau of Investigation and other federal agencies. Law enforcement and police-type occupations had also intrigued Bill and his interest increased as the patient continued to describe the FBI. The patient advised Bill that if he was interested in such a career he should obtain a degree in accounting or law. While still in the Air Force Bill wrote to Roosevelt University in Chicago for their accounting curriculum and the name of the textbooks then in use. He arranged to have the textbooks shipped to him, which he read religiously during his leisure hours. Roosevelt University informed him that because of his prior educational background he would need only 28 or 30 hours in accounting and about thirty hours in related subjects. Bill stated that when he was discharged from the military, "I was ready."

He enrolled in Roosevelt University and subsequently graduated with a Bachelor of Science degree in accounting in September 1957. He also attended Chicago-Kent College of Law for one year. After graduating from Roosevelt University he learned that the Internal Revenue Service was seeking applicants for the Internal Revenue Agent position. He applied and was accepted.

Chapter Eighteen

When Bill applied for the Internal Revenue Agent position it was not necessary to take a written examination as it had been in earlier years. A grade average in college was the primary criterion used in determining an applicant's acceptability to the Service. He was interviewed by a panel and accepted, but was not brought on board until the beginning of the next fiscal year beginning July 1958.

His internal revenue agent training spanned six months and was conducted at the John Marshall Law School facilities. Bill stated that there were 33 students and he ranked first in the class. The training consisted of three months in the classroom and three months on-the-job training, accompanying senior agents in the field. During this training, District Director H. Alan Long visited the classroom and told them that the Intelligence Division was seeking applicants for three special agent positions. An Intelligence Division representative who accompanied the District Director described the duties of special agents and the mission of the division. Bill indicated that when he initially accepted the internal revenue agent position he thought that those duties encompassed the job just described by the Intelligence Division official. He thought to himself, "I'm in the wrong division." He applied for a special agent position and was accepted before he had an opportunity to perform any duties as an internal revenue agent.

Chapter Nineteen

Subsequent to applying for a special agent position Bill was interviewed in depth by a panel of Intelligence Division officials. Neither his education nor the internal revenue agent training were in question and the interviewers advised that they would concentrate on his personal background, i.e., integrity, dependability, many "what if" situations, and his "meet and deal" qualities. Also, Bill was advised that as the first African-American special agent in the Chicago District and the Midwest Region he was certain to encounter racial slurs or problems and was asked how he would handle them. Based on their line of questioning and comments, they apparently were not aware of the fact that there were several other African-American special agents already on board. According to Bill, in about a week or so he was advised that he had been selected for the position. Ironically, he was assigned to the group supervisor who had addressed his internal revenue agent training class, and this person was to become his mentor. Bill had nothing but praise for this person and felt that, "He saved my neck probably on more occasions than I care to remember." This supervisor had it all: patience, protectiveness, ability to transfer his talents to the agents under his supervision, and the uncanny ability to guide and to advise without using a forceful manner. Bill stated that, "As a result of this environment, I really busted my butt for him. Promotions came fast and others in our group congratulated me on my many successes. There was no animosity because of my race." They would say, "You got it faster than anyone, and you deserved it." Bill stated that his philosophy was, and still is, "When you have the youth, go for it. Don't wait until you are old and expect to do great things. That's not possible. It's downhill, never up." With that philosophy always in mind he submitted the best cases, most cases, and the best reports. To him, that combination spelled nothing but success and recognition.

With Internal Revenue Agent training already completed his next formal training was in Washington, D.C. at the Treasury Law Enforcement Officers' Training School.

Bill vividly recalled the six-week training course at 712-4th Street N.W., Washington, D.C. After all these years he recalled the layout of the building as well as one of the lead instructors, J.T.L. Stemple. He also recalled that he ranked very high in his class and had no difficulty ingesting the subject matter. He was the only African-American special agent in the class. Even more than the events taking place in the classroom and training exercises, he recalled a city of cleanliness, tranquility, and a feeling of pride in being a part of the federal establishment, with a new pocket commission and a gold badge. He walked the streets at night and visited the neighborhood movie houses without fear of violence. His final comment about the six weeks in Washington was, "I loved it, I loved it."

His next school was the Special Agents' Basic School that was also conducted in the Washington, D.C. Internal Revenue Service building in 1960. The building was not air-conditioned at the time and those six weeks of training were miserable, but he still enjoyed the city. It was as beautiful as ever. He did not encounter any classroom difficulties and upon completion of this training he returned to his Chicago post of duty.

He remembered many of his successful prosecution cases, too numerous to cite here, but two of the more memorable are included to illustrate the complexities, variety, and difficulties encountered everyday by the agents in the field.

First Criminal Case

Armless Whiz—Whiz Man
d/b/a Whiz Movement, Inc.

On December 27, 1963 a federal District Court judge sentenced A. Robert Leggett (not real name of person or organization) to prison for a period of two years on each of fourteen counts to run concurrently. The taxpayer, about fifty-five to sixty years of age, was a double amputee, both arms having been lost in an accident when he was seventeen years of age. With the use of artificial limbs, he was reputed to write well, type more than forty words per minute (publicized in *Believe It or Not*, by Ripley), shaved and otherwise care for himself without assistance.

The case originated as a result of numerous complaints received from taxpayers that Leggett prepared their income tax returns and caused their respective refund checks to be delivered to the Whiz Movement, Inc., a membership organization founded by Leggett that provided accounting, tax and legal services to its members.

It was determined from testimony of numerous witnesses that Leggett, through various forms of trickery, obtained powers of attorney from these taxpayers that authorized him to negotiate their refund checks and use the cash proceeds. The witnesses also testified that Leggett listed false and fictitious exemptions and deductions on their 1960 and 1961 tax returns.

In order to determine whether the allegations were true, that Leggett was in the business of preparing fraudulent tax returns, four agents were assigned to act in an undercover capacity as tax clients. They gave Leggett information and asked him to prepare 1961 tax returns for them. In three of the four assignments, the agents were equipped with a recording device. Their respective interviews corroborated the testimony of Leggett's tax clients.

Leggett organized this allegedly non-profit organization in 1955 for the sole purpose of preparing tax returns and obtaining the respective refund checks. Leggett required that anyone who wanted his or her tax return prepared become a member of the Whiz Movement and give it a power of attorney. Consequently, becoming a member of the Movement was tantamount to authorizing the Movement to negotiate the refund check. Even before the formation of the Whiz Movement, Leggett was in the business of preparing returns and receiving the clients' refund checks.

After the client completed the application to become a member of the movement, he was interviewed by Leggett, who gained the confidence of his taxpayer client by 'knocking' the Internal Revenue Service. He told them that they (tax clients) were forced to file the short simple form in prior years, thereby not taking advantage of their correct deductions. At this point Leggett often asked the clients if they had received a refund in prior years; if not, Leggett suggested that he would file the necessary amended tax returns for the client and get a refund, which would be divided fifty/fifty.

Leggett asked the tax clients numerous questions concerning exemptions and deductions. In regard to exemptions, a number of witnesses testified that Leggett fraudulently placed one or more questionable or fictitious exemptions on their tax returns. Furthermore, he attempted to convince the tax clients that they were married to their girlfriends; that they were still married to their divorced wives, or that they had a fictitious child. For instance, Leggett would ask, "Are you married?"

Tax client: "No."

Leggett responded, "Yes you are."

After the questioning period was completed, Leggett requested the tax client to sign his name at least three times—once on a blank Form 1040, and twice on a long four-page worksheet, known as a deposition, on which Leggett listed all the exemptions and deductions claimed on the tax return filed with the Internal Revenue Service. This deposition was used exclusively by two accountants who physically prepared the tax returns for the Whiz Movement members. As previously stated, the tax client was required to sign the deposition twice: (1) A section declaring under the penalty of perjury that exemptions and deductions as set forth thereon were correct; and (2) a power of attorney section that authorized the Whiz Movement to receive and negotiate the refund checks. However, Leggett used trickery in obtaining these signatures. He stacked these forms in a pile, with Form 1040 on the top.

Leggett ensured receipt by him of the refund checks by listing his address on each tax return, and also by completely eliminating the correct address of his tax clients on the accompanying Form W-2. Since Leggett blotted out the address of the witnesses, it was extremely difficult to locate them. Most of the witnesses had common names and were transients. If they were located, in most cases they would go to Leggett and he would tell them not to talk to the Revenue Service; that he (Leggett) would take care of everything.

Leggett deceived his tax clients relative to the correct refund due. In many cases Leggett gave his tax clients a "copy" of their respective income tax return. This copy which listed the correct address of the client, disclosed a lesser refund than that shown on the original tax return filed by Leggett with the Internal Revenue Service. In a number of cases, the refund on the original return was $200 to $300 greater than the refund on the copy given to the tax client. Leggett's three bank accounts disclosed that he had deposited thousands of dollars in refund checks during the period 1960 through 1961.

Retired Special Agent Mannie advised that two internal revenue agents cooperated in the lengthy joint investigation. Leggett, the armless whiz but effective tax expert, was convicted on 14 counts of preparing false and fraudulent tax returns for others.

The federal judge sentenced Leggett to prison for two years on each of fourteen counts to run concurrently.

Leggett had appealed to juries for sympathy because of his handicap, but this jury was unmoved by his antics.

Biggest Case—Most Interesting Case

Dr. Marcus Mercenary

The Brothers Mercenary, Marcus and Marcel, (not their real names), were _____ citizens by way of Argentina; and were naturalized by a Special Act of Congress. This case originated as a result of an editorial appearing in a big-city newspaper wherein it was disclosed that Dr. Mercenary sold a substance or drug called "Sure Cure" (pseudonym), an anti-cancer cure for about $10.00 an ampule. He earned millions selling this drug to cancer victims; nonetheless, it appeared that this 'drug' was nothing but mineral oil.

The Mercenarys claimed that they escaped the Nazis by way of the Vatican. They alleged that they had spent millions in developing this drug during the years after arriving in North America in the early 1940s; that since they are now selling these ampules they wanted to recover their high research and development cost on their tax returns with no proof of actually incurring or spending millions to develop the alleged drug. As a result of using this development costing millions, one of the brothers offset his entire profit on his tax return; therefore paying no income tax whatsoever.

The investigation was conducted in part by IRS' International Operations and in North America by Bill Mannie and a cooperating agent.

In a foreign country, IRS agents were able to trace millions deposited, and subsequently transferred to as Swiss bank.

At the time it was illegal for American citizens to buy gold; however, the Mercenarys purchased a small fortune of gold bullion and failed to report thousands in interest income.

The witnesses from a foreign country, who were stockholders in the laboratory that allegedly produced the drug, stated that the Mercenarys never spent millions in developing the drug. They allegedly made the investment which was a nominal amount.

During the 1950s and early 1960s, the drug was the most popular anti-cancer drug in the United States, even though controversial. However, it was only sold in the State of _____; consequently, cancer patients were required to come to that state to be examined by a doctor in order to receive a supply of the drug.

In the 1960s, the Brothers Mercenary were prosecuted under Title 18 USC regarding the efficacy of alleged drug. The investigation was conducted by the Food and Drug Administration. The subsequent trial generated substantial publicity locally and nationally. After a protracted trial of six months, the Mercenarys were found not guilty. As rapidly as possible, one of the Mercenarys obtained his seized passport and fled the United States.

In the late 1960s, a complaint was filed in the United States District Court, against Dr. Mercenary for violation of 26 USC 7201, Income Tax Evasion. The United States Marshal Office held the warrant for his arrest.

The civil taxes and penalties total millions.

Chapter Twenty

As will often happen with many special agents who had a very successful career in the field, they are approached by management regarding their career plans. Bill's group supervisor approached him on more than one occasion to feel him out as to his interests and finally suggested that Bill submit a formal statement that he had an interest in a first-line supervisory position. The supervisor reasoned that Bill had many good qualities that he could pass on to agents in his group. This would benefit not only the special agents but the Service even more so. Bill advised his supervisor that he was happy working cases and the freedom that only agents in the field can enjoy. He was reluctant to give up that position which many of us feel is the best job in the Service: a bag-carrying GS-13, with a vehicle, many times on premium pay, and with little or no supervision. However, after the "for the good of the Service" routine from his supervisor, and remembering his supervisor's help when he was a new agent, Bill finally relented, applied for, and was elevated to a group supervisor position, reluctantly leaving his group buddies behind. Bill stated that he never regretted his decision to become a supervisor.

His group amassed an impressive record of successful prosecutions and he was again approached and asked to take over a trainee group. The division was in disarray, and undergoing an internal reorganization. He was the junior group supervisor and new special agents coming on board desperately needed "The Bill Mannie approach." He hated to lose his group, but agreed to set up the trainee group program with the help of three senior special agents to act as coaches. He was given carte blanche in hiring. They visited local campuses and interviewed hundreds of potential applicants, including about 20 Blacks. From that group of persons interviewed he recall hiring a soft-spoken, highly intelligent African-American female. She was the first female to become a special agent in the Midwest Region, which included the Chicago District. The hiring of females came about because of a strongly worded directive from the Civil Service Commission in 1971 that left no doubt anyone using a person's sex to hire or failure to hire, "had no place in the government." Bill indicated that he never regretted hiring Ms. _____. She was an aggressive and effective agent and eventually left Chicago for higher grades and better positions.

Bill recalled being involved with the assistant division chief in starting the Tax Fraud Investigative Aid program. Originally those employees were referred to as Enforcement Technicians. Their duties were formalized, expanded, and their title changed to Tax Fraud Investigative Aid (TFIA), This program was very successful and resulted in a career ladder for semiprofessionals.

When asked whether he considered the Internal Revenue Service an equal opportunity employer, Bill was emphatic, "Yes, it's not the Service's fault for the lack of Blacks."

During his recruiting, which dates back to 1961, he stated that the GS-5 starting salary was too low. The civil rights movement created jobs previously not available to minorities and government positions were not attractive to college graduates still undecided regarding their careers.

Bill believed that he could have advanced to any position to which he aspired, but he limited his availability to the Chicago District. His personnel papers disclosed that as far back as 1963 he declined a transfer to Washington, D.C., and reiterated in his 1972 stance, his lack of availability outside the Chicago District. He advised this writer, who attempted on more than one occasion to bring Bill to Washington, D.C. or to accept a promotion elsewhere, that his reasons for remaining in Chicago were strictly personal. I asked him to explain. He stated that during his first year of marriage his wife joined him while he was serving in the military and he promised her that he would never leave her to raise their family alone. He kept that promise and spent his entire career from 1958 through 1984 in the Chicago District, where, I might add, he established an impressive record of service.

He was respected not only in the Service but also throughout the federal establishment and was selected one year as a Finalist in the Federal Employee of the Year Award.

This respect for Bill as a special agent and as a professional carried over to his post-retirement endeavors.

During my interview with Bill I asked him what he considered his greatest success in the Service. He pondered this question and surprisingly did not describe any personal accomplishments.

In his view, visiting college campuses on recruiting assignments, hiring young men and women to special agent positions, training them and nurturing their careers; and finally, seeing them move up the career ladder was most fulfilling to him. This logic reinforces the self-portrait of William Edward Mannie.

He spoke emotionally of one of his trainees. Dick Wassanaar, who later served as a coach in his trainee group and also a personal friend. Wassanaar eventually attained the highest position in the Criminal Investigation Division-Assistant Commissioner and served in that position from 1982 until his death in 1986. It was great personal loss to Bill.

Naturally, the next question to Bill referred to his failures and/or disappointments during his career. Again, he pondered the question and finally responded by saying that he personally had no disappointments, because he advanced as fast and as far as he desired, considering his limited mobility as to locations. However, his disappointments came when special agents in the division had difficulties being promoted above the journeyman (GS-11) grade. He surmised that many agents came on board at the end of World War II and most retired about the same time, necessitating massive hiring. This practice resulted in many excellent agents later competing for the few GS-12 and GS-13 positions available. However, he agreed that this problem was not unique to the Chicago District, because budgetary constraints and the makeup of district offices created problems throughout the Service. Regardless of the reasons, failure to receive promotions was very demoralizing and a serious problem for management, but things seem to work out in the long run. Bill considered keeping the agents highly motivated a difficult task, at best.

Bill's private papers disclosed that two years before he was eligible for retirement he was contemplating his future. An insight into his thoughts were found in a memorandum to district officials titled, "Retention of Enforcement Credential and Badge." The text of that memorandum was as follows:

To: _____
From: William E. Mannie Group Manager
Subject: Retention of Enforcement Credential and Badge
Appointment as a Special Agent

On July 7, 1958, I reported to duty as an Internal Revenue Agent GS-5. During the latter part of 1958, Chicago's first District Director, H. Alan Long, was seeking African-American special agents for the Intelligence Division. After completion of my six months training as a revenue agent, I was selected on January 12, 1959 as the first African-American special agent in the Chicago District. When I entered on duty as a special agent, there were only three African-American special agents with the Intelligence Division nationwide; Hilton Owens out of Cleveland, Ohio whom I knew and first met via telephone, and two others in New York.

High Crime Area

Almost immediately I was involved in all types of investigations in the high crime area that is my neighborhood. Because of the possible danger involved, I was always armed. It is significant to realize that during this period, our investigative efforts were very limited in these areas in Chicago because of the rapid emerging of the civil rights movement and civil strife in the African-American community in general.

With my accession, the Intelligence Division was able to successfully prosecute the legendary Armless Worker, _____ _____ a double amputee, having lost both his arms as a teenager. _____ was the most notorious false return preparer in the Chicago District. The Secret Service had tried to prosecute him three times, yet failed each time. The State attempted to prosecute him numerous times, yet they also failed. In order to successfully prosecute _____, I reviewed all court records relative to the many reasons why _____ was never successfully prosecuted; there were never enough qualified witnesses to testify effectively against him. I interviewed over two hundred taxpayer/clients living in this high crime area in order to make this first successful case against _____. He was subsequently convicted and sentenced to three years in Sandstone.

To this day, on many occasions, I can be anywhere in my southside neighborhood, on the street, in a store, at a theater, or even in church, when someone will walk up to me and say, "Are you Special Agent Mannie?" "You're Mr. Mannie with the IRS" . . . "Aren't you the FBI agent who worked on so and so?" "Don't you remember interviewing me. I remember you, I was in the place when you raided it."

Gambling Investigations

I was never assigned to the gambling group because of my other key investigations yet I was involved in a joint project with the Chicago Police Department dealing with African-American policy operators. During the early 1960s, I was assigned to learn and develop information relative to policy operations in the African-American area. I was detailed to work with three African-American police officers who were assigned to the Chicago Police Department Gambling Unit working out of Washington Park on 53rd and Cottage Grove. This unit was part of the Chicago Police Department Intelligence Division. Since this is my residential area, I was recognized on numerous occasions by persons who knew me from school, the neighborhood, etc. When I became a special agent, it was "Well Mannie, one of our brothers has made it."

Starting in 1959, I have been on numerous gambling raids conducted by the Intelligence Division. A large number of these raids occurred in the African-American areas on the south and west sides of Chicago. Since we had only two African-American special agents in the Chicago District during most of the 1960s, invariably I was the only minority special agent in the raiding party. Unfortunately, I was recognized on several occasions. Just recently, on June 15, 1978, I was a raid leader when we raided numerous betting messenger services. My location was in a high crime area on East 71st Street in Chicago. This location was exactly two blocks east of my sister-in-law's residence.

Case Development Activity

As a result of this early contact with the Gambling Unit of the CPD, I have developed contacts with these African-American police officers which can be invaluable in developing leads to possible tax violations. In the near future, I anticipate renewing these sources of information.

Minority Recruitment and Contacts

I have been recruiting for the Internal Revenue Service generally, and the Intelligence Division specifically, since 1961. I have been engaged in numerous minority recruitment projects where my enforcement commission and badge were actually instrumental in convincing the candidates of the positive opportunities available to minorities in federal law enforcement as a career.

During the 1970s, I personally was instrumental in locating and recruiting four of our topflight special agents.

In order to convince these candidates, it was necessary for me to first actually prove to their placement officials that the opportunities for minorities as special agents were not a façade. They requested to see and inspect my federal commission and badge. They asked me for a brief history of my own employment and progress as a special agent. They wanted to know what were the opportunities available now for additional African-American special agents; whether there was a quota system for minorities, etc. I had no difficulty in answering any questions regarding opportunities since I am the first product. I feel extremely comfortable in this type of recruitment because the best will definitely be successful. This is my first love and one of my strong areas. I would like to continue these contacts as often as possible in order to build a repertoire of minority candidates for future hiring opportunities as special agents.

It is a proven fact that the most important thing that initially impresses the prospective African-American special agent candidate is our badge and credentials. When I go to the college or university placement office to recruit minorities, they invariably want to see my enforcement commission and badge. They use me as an example of the possibilities their students will have as special agents. These placement officers are usually minorities themselves and are extremely protective. I have had a number of these placement officers say, "We just want to be sure you are the real thing and not someone who was reading a recruitment flyer relative to the position."

I definitely recall on several occasions as I was giving a recruitment presentation to a group of students and their instructors when someone would ask to see our "famous badge and commission" that they saw flashed on TV or in the movies. Chicago State University, which is in my neighborhood, is definitely an excellent school to recruit African-American candidates. We have been very successful here, hiring four special agents.

I have an exceptional contact with personnel in the business department of the university.

It has been my experience that to effectively recruit minority students, they must see a symbol or proof that another minority has definitely "made it." With my credential and badge, I will be able to show them, first, that I am in fact a special agent and, second, that I am a supervisory special agent and not just a minority employee of the Internal Revenue Service.

I sincerely believe that it is extremely important that I retain my badge and credential as a positive identification media while recruiting minority special agents and any other official contact with the African-American community in general. Reality will indicate that I do represent a symbol for other potential minority candidates. Furthermore, I am extremely familiar with the high crime area and the African-American community. I definitely would like to continue to keep my present contacts in the minority schools and community and develop additional contacts, which will definitely be beneficial to the Service.

There are numerous additional reasons why the retention of my enforcement commission and badge are necessary, such as:

1. Surveillance conducted by my group and others;
2. Arrest situations—in 1972 and 1973, my group alone arrested 31 tax preparers;
3. Case development in the high crime area (there are a number of tax violators out there);
4. Accompanying my special agents on interviews in the high crime areas (especially the project housing developments) and normal visitations with special agents assigned to my group;
5. To participate as raid leader on gambling raids, especially in the high crime area where the area is all African-American; and,
6. My group is listed as Group 20 in the "Chicago District Office Telephone Directory" under Emergency Service." I have participated with a firearm in emergency situations with the Examination and Taxpayer Service on numerous occasions. Presently, I have 21 months to go before I will be eligible to retire. Based on the aforementioned situations,

I respectfully request that I be permitted to retain my commission and badge.

s/William E. Mannie"

Bill's memorandum, addressed to his superior, was answered with one word: "Approved."

After Retirement

Chicago—September 26, 1984

Mayor Washington Monday appointed the city's first Black chief investigator for the law department in addition to a new director of labor relations. Washington appointed William E. Mannie, 53, who has had 30 years experience with the federal government. He will supervise 20 investigators in the law department and will make $39,000 annually. Prior to his appointment, Mannie worked for the Internal Revenue Service (IRS) as a supervisor in the criminal investigation division. He spent three years in the U.S. Air Force and retired from his IRS position in January of this year. A graduate of Roosevelt University, Mannie received his Bachelor's degree in accounting in 1959.

Bill confirmed that as Director of Legal Investigations, Department of Law, for the City of Chicago, he was responsible for the conduct of investigations relating to suits filed against the City of Chicago. His department's findings were presented to city officials for use in defending the city and protecting the city government's interests. He displayed as much enthusiasm about this job as he did in the Internal Revenue Service.

PART III

Frederick L. Sleet

The first African-American special agent to become an Assistant Regional Commissioner, the second highest position in the Criminal Investigation Division.

Foreword

I had known Fred Sleet since he first joined the Intelligence Division in 1962. We became very good friends in the ensuing years, in constant contact seeking each other's council, advice, and sympathy.

We both had our highs and lows over the years and I am totally familiar with Fred's good and bad times, and there were many. Fred made it to the very top of our profession. There were times he almost quit, but my advice to Fred when he was at his lowest was, "Fred, just hang in there." I knew he could. He did.

If this document is sometimes less than objective, I apologize, but the truth speaks for itself regardless of how emotional it may be presented. Herein lies the saga of complex Fred.

Chapter Twenty-One

Introduction

Fred was born in New Castle, Indiana in 1928, about forty miles from Indianapolis. The family later moved to his father's hometown, Connersville, Indiana, about fifty six miles from Indianapolis, where he was reared and attended secondary schools.

Fred was number six in a family of 17 children, who grew up in the Great Depression years. His father had a federal Works Progress Administration (WPA) job, as well as other odd jobs and "did not start to make any money until World War II."

In his own words, Fred described those years as follows,

"From an African-American family of 17 children in a sleepy little town in Central Indiana in the early 1930s I rose to the second highest position in the Criminal Investigation Division, Internal Revenue Service.

I was the sixth child of seventeen in the family and we were a very close-knitted family but very individualistic.

My parents' main struggle in the 1930s and 1940s was to provide the necessities of life (food, clothing and shelter). Difficult at best, but successful as to proof.

Of the seventeen children, fifteen lived to reach majority and all at least graduated, mostly with honors, from the town's only high school.

My educational experience was very unique and special in that in our small town the dreams of a child were void of color, which was an oddity because of the (racial) adversities at the time. Many of my peers went on to become doctors, dentists, attorneys, schoolteachers, and other professionals. The mix educational experience at that time did not seem to leave permanent scars on the inner self other than dealing and coping with the times.

I remember my father as a man who was rich in pride and quiet principles with high morals and intellectual convictions.

I realized later in life that he must have cried in silence because he could not provide for us in a way he wanted, although he did his best with odd jobs and the Works Progress Administration, a federal works program. At worst, he was a strict disciplinarian, and at best, instinctively, a loving man whose strength was just being there in a supportive role for his entire brood. My mother was a woman meant to have children. She was tender, loving, and caring. She died at age 45 and I hope she has looked down on me and smiled with a thought, "I knew he could."

My public school accomplishments were minimally average because I actually thought of myself as being somewhat demented because of a physical handicap that created in me a sense of inferiority. I did not realize my capabilities until I joined the military. Upon graduating from high school the future looked bleak insofar as employment was concerned. I had a job with a dry cleaning establishment that paid fifty cents per hour. That was in 1948, and as I observed the GIs returning from the military service, I knew of the GI Bill for college and the military would be my salvation. I enlisted in the army at the age of seventeen to the dismay of my parents who never thought I would pass the physical examination. As a small child I had the rickets and did not walk until I was five years of age. I was supposed to be an invalid, so I was an invalid until I decided to make it on my own. I certainly had a very sympathetic medical examiner because he asked me, "Son, do you really want to join the Army?" to which I answered in my strongest voice, "Yes sir." No one could believe that I, this little guy with a limp, passed the medical examination, and even more unbelievable was that the real reason for enlisting was to obtain the GI Bill benefits. The Army experience was painful to me and I hated every day of it. I recall having one thousand days to serve and that seemed like forever.

For some unknown reason I took shorthand and typing (very unusual for a person of ethnic background) and I literally typed my way through those one thousand days.

I took about one and one-half weeks of an eight-week basic training course and was placed in the office as an administrative clerk. I skipped the regular technical training and went directly to the Advanced Administrative School and completed the course at the top of the class. After spending about one year stateside and two years in Japan, I was honorably discharged and entered college. That was in 1949. I entered in Butler University, Indianapolis, Indiana, but from a small town, the campus environment was too large and too impersonal. Also, my college preparation was very weak. I transferred to Anderson College, Anderson, Indiana, a school with eight or nine hundred students, where I was consistently on the dean's list. Had I remained at Butler University, I would probably have flunked out. I graduated in 1953 with a Bachelor of Science degree with an accounting major. I was finally somebody."

I asked Fred to explain what he meant by "I was finally somebody." He explained, that because of his affliction (rickets) he was unable to walk until he was five years of age, and was taken to the hospital by his mother at least once per week. If he was supposed to be an invalid, then he would be an invalid. His brothers and sisters were good musicians and good students in school, while he just went through the motions. It was only after the barrage of tests he took upon entering the military did he realize that "This kid may have something after all." His test scores compared to an IQ of 135, and it was reflected in the assignments he received. After only about one week of basic training he was assigned to assistant company clerk duties. Later, after attending an administrative school, he received an administrative Military Occupational Specialty, commonly referred to as MOS, which was normally assigned to the high-ranking non-commissioned officers, and he was still a private. After completing his tour of duty in Japan, everyday of which he hated, he returned home and enrolled in college.

While in college and thereafter Fred worked as a floor sweeper at General Motors in Anderson, Indiana. He was in good company there. He jokingly stated that the sweepers were probably the most educated group of laborers in the country—African-Americans with bachelor's and master's degrees. As to why he chose accounting as his major in college he stated that he was probably naïve at the time. During secondary school, students were not African-American or white, just students. He was "always good with figures and accounting was a natural." He knew while growing up that there were certain things that blacks could not do, but his father had always told him to do what you desire, and always do your very best. Fred stated. "I followed his advice."

Upon graduating from Anderson College in 1953 with an accounting degree, he learned the hard, cruel facts of life. There was no place in the accounting profession in Indiana for a African-American person. He recalled asking one of his accounting professors for a job, any job. He was told, "Fred, I can't hire you. I would lose all of my clients." So much for the accounting profession. Fred continued to work as a sweeper at General Motors.

On one occasion when visiting the Post Office he observed a poster stating that the Internal Revenue Service was seeking applicants for Internal Revenue Agent positions at a salary of $3,410. In May 1955 Fred began his 25 year career with the Internal Revenue Service.

Notice of Personnel Actions

Action	Effective	Grade	Position
Appointment	May, 55	5	Internal Revenue Agent
Promotion	Jan-29-56	7	Internal Revenue Agent
Promotion	Apr-21-57	9	Internal Revenue Agent
Promotion	May-17-59	11	Internal Revenue Agent
Reassignment	Jan-7-62	11	Special Agent
Reassignment	Jan. 1963	11	Internal Revenue Agent
Reassignment	Jul-21-63	11	Special Agent
Promotion	Aug-29-65	12	Special Agent
Promotion	Mar 70	13	Special Agent
Promotion		13	Group Supervisor
Promotion	Dec-8-74	14	Assistant Chief
Promotion	Aug-28-77	15	Chief
Promotion	Aug-10-80	ES4	Assistant Regional Commissioner—CI
Retirement	Jan-3-83		

Chapter Twenty-Two

As Fred recalled, the civil service examination for the internal revenue agent's position was not difficult. The interview by a panel of officials seemed to be a formality. It appeared to Fred at the time that he had been selected and had only to formally accept the GS-5 position in Anderson, Indiana at $3,410. He accepted. His supervisor advised him that he would be the first African-American internal revenue agent in Anderson and he might have problems.

Fred informed his supervisor that he was now a federal agent, with credentials to prove it; he would perform his duties to the best of his abilities, but he would not tolerate any disrespect from anyone, whether it came from inside or outside the Service. He indicated that if he was not respected by his superiors, peers, or the taxpaying public, it never came to his attention.

In the Audit Division, he was promoted from GS-5 to GS-11, going from $3,410 to $7,030, but was not happy. When asked why not, he stated, "Happiness was not related to the job." He was a success as an internal revenue agent, but that was how it was suppose to be. He had to prove he could be, and was, a success at any endeavor he undertook.

As a revenue agent his completed cases placed him as a top performer in that division even when he first joined and was in training.

While success in the Audit Division came with relative ease, Fred's fondness for police-type work was apparent. After graduating from college with an accounting degree he had an interest in becoming an FBI agent, but was advised at the time that agents were required to be certified public accountants or attorneys.

During his tour in the Service as an internal revenue agent, there were occasions when he discovered "badges of fraud" during audits, whereupon he referred the matter to the Intelligence Division. He recalled that the first case he referred to the Intelligence Division culminated in a successful prosecution.

Chapter Twenty-Three

In 1960 or 1961 Fred contacted the Chief, Intelligence Division, Indianapolis regarding a special agent position. He could not recall whether this occurred in 1960 or 1961, but he recalled the conversation;

> Chief: "If you become a special agent, where do you want to be assigned?"
> Fred: "Indianapolis."
> Chief: "You can't come here. You've got to go to Gary."
> Fred: "No."
> Chief: "You're wasting my time."

Fred recalled that the chief, in a swivel chair, literally turned his back. Fred's first attempt to become a special agent was a dismal failure. As he looked back on the incident and gave the chief the benefit of the doubt, it maybe that there were no vacancies in Indianapolis at the time. This particular chief retired shortly thereafter. Enter Joseph C. Hilgenberg, the new chief, and believed by Fred, to ever be his nemesis. Hilgenberg, a native Hoosier, began his Intelligence Division career in 1945.

Fred conferred with Hilgenberg and the conversation went along the same line as Fred's conversation with the prior chief, but Hilgenberg seemed to Fred to be an honorable man. Fred accepted the position, with Gary, Indiana as his post of duty, after being assured by Hilgenberg that after a year or so he could return to Indianapolis. With that assurance Fred joined the Intelligence Division on January 7, 1962 as a GS-11 special agent, the same grade he held in the Audit Division. At that time his salary was $7,820 per year. On January 19, 1962, less than two weeks after joining the Intelligence Division, Fred was shipped out to work undercover. "Undercover, what's that?" Fred asked. Regional officials in Cincinnati, Ohio advised Fred that he would be "obtaining probable cause for search/arrest warrants on an illegal numbers lottery." "Probable who, for an illegal what?" Fred inquired. The IRS officials, after their initial shock that Fred was not street wise, briefly explained what was needed. It was obvious to Fred that they assumed that he, like Owens and Patterson, with whom they had dealt in the past, was familiar with the numbers lotteries and what was needed. After all, didn't all African-Americans know about gambling and all its machinations? This was Fred's first exposure to "blackism" in the Service. It should be noted that this was not some form of racial discrimination. The reality was that the lucrative illegal numbers racket was operated on a daily basis by African-Americans, but was bankrolled by whites. It was virtually impossible to connect, sufficient for use in criminal proceedings in district court, the numbers bankers, who were well-insulated from the daily operations. That was always of primary concern and it required the use of American-American undercover agents to accomplish this task.

Fred drove to a southern Ohio town with his pocket commission, gold badge, and a.38 Smith & Wesson, in his personal vehicle, bearing Indiana license plates traceable directly to Special Agent Frederick L. Sleet. A big mistake. With no knowledge of baseball, basketball or football tickets, and even less knowledge of numbers lotteries, Fred made another mistake. He confided in the town drunk, who eagerly agreed to assist him in getting the information needed. Shortly after receiving assurances from his helper Fred began to receive cold stares, total avoidance, and a feeling of being unwelcome in that town. He indicated that, "They ran me out of town. I was hot. The police never discourteous, but actually followed me to the edge of town to make sure I actually left. Man, I was hot, and scared."

He had no opportunity to return home and check on his family. He was told to proceed to Norfolk, Virginia for his next assignment. Same thing—a numbers lottery. After several months in Norfolk, he moved on to Middletown, Ohio; then on to Hampton, Virginia. Success came there. He returned to Gary in December 1962. His first year in the Intelligence Division was totally undercover except for six weeks training at the Treasury Law Enforcement Officers' Training School in Washington, D.C., and also an opportunity to observe the "Screw" Andrews criminal tax trial in Kentucky.

Returning to Gary in December 1962, Fred asked his immediate supervisor to confer with the division chief regarding being transferred to Indianapolis as promised. The chief advised Fred, through the group supervisor, that the transfer would not be forthcoming for another two or three years. Fred indicated that he was dumbfounded and went on annual leave to cool off. Shortly thereafter, he transferred back to the Audit Division in his former internal revenue agent position, a very bitter man. Almost thirty years later that bitterness remained.

As Fred related it, he had worked hard in college, made the dean's list and graduated. He was a well-respected professional, only to be returned to ghettos, live in roach-infested hotel rooms, eating in "greasy spoon" restaurants, and living the most miserable and dangerous life one can imagine. That was not why he had joined the Intelligence Division.

While back in the Audit Division Fred was contacted by a very close special agent friend and advised that the Intelligence Division desperately wanted him back. He knew that this message did not come from his old nemesis, the chief. He was further advised to contact the Assistant Regional Commissioner—Intelligence, Thomas P. McGovern, which he did. As he recalled the conversation went as follows:

> McGovern: "What would it take to get you to transfer back to the Intelligence Division?"
> Fred: "That's easy. Indianapolis post of duty and a chance to work regular cases, not only undercover assignments."
> McGovern: "That's all?"
> Fred: "Yes."
> McGovern: "Done. Does Hilgenberg know why you left?"
> Fred: "Yes, everybody knows."
> McGovern: "Welcome home."

A short time later Fred received a telephone call from the Intelligence Division asking him when could he report for duty in Indianapolis.

The division chief was completely bypassed in this maneuver, for which, according to Fred, he was never forgiven. That was primarily Fred's reason for calling the chief his nemesis.

Again, Fred's career took off. He was permitted to conduct income tax cases, and undercover assignments did not stop, but became infrequent. As to his success rate of prosecutions, Fred stated, "If they (special agents) had one, I had two or three." There were times when he had five or more prosecution cases in the U.S. Attorney's office awaiting trial.

In a molded and mildewed carton, I scanned numerous newspaper articles, yellowed with age, and selected a few at random to illustrate the diversity of the investigations successfully completed by Fred.

Newspaper Articles

"Physician Sentenced to 2 years, Fined $22,500 For Tax Evasion.

Despite a two-hour plea by his attorney and witnesses, Dr. _____ 61-year-old physician, yesterday was sentenced to two years in prison and fined $22,500 in Federal Court for evading $84,294.11 in income taxes."

"Couple Arrested in Tax Case.

An _____ couple, owners of a seat cover store, were arrested yesterday on a Federal grand jury indictment charging they dodged $27,765.08 in income taxes for 1957, 1958 and 1959.

"IRS Makes a Pinch in Own Office. His job as 'Numbering.'

The Internal Revenue Service blushed a little today, then announced it had arrested an alleged numbers racket operator in its own office."

"Quits Federal Job"

Man allegedly failed to Purchase Stamp. Internal Revenue agents have Arrested _____ 42, on a charge of accepting numbers bets without having a $50 federal tax stamp . . . The resignation was accepted yesterday by his employer—the Baltimore district of the Internal Revenue Service.

"Convict one, release one in policy trial — longtime policy wheel operator, was found guilty in U.S. District Court here this morning on 11 counts of understating rackets income in 1967 and 1968 by almost $2 million. Charges against_____ also of aiding . . . were dismissed by Judge_____, who said the government hadn't furnished enough evidence to support the charges . . . I have strong suspicions_____ is guilty, but there was no evidence."

"Daughter in Dog House _ An extra Buck or Two Brings IRS Cur-Tail. There was only one problem with claiming Cindy as an exemption. Cindy Louise was _____'s dog, Uncle Sam Says."

I also gave Fred the almost impossible task of remembering his first criminal case, and when asked, hesitated, "Most certainly." I put him on the spot again and asked if he remembered his largest and most interesting cases. What follows, in his own words, are his best recollections

The very first criminal case I worked was on the doctor (abortionist) that I told you about. It was investigated twice before by the division (one by a special agent who later became a group manager) and by the then chief. Both were closed with minimal civil adjustments, although _____ did get a signed net worth, which I used as a starting point.

This case was my very first and with the havoc I caused by coming back I think they (management) were attempting to try my mettle.

The doctor dealt primarily in margin stock accounts (33) where money shifted back and forth between accounts, dividend deposited and interest earned, investments in street name, wife's maiden name, children, and a brother who lived in _____,_____.

The gross investment was $1.8 million.

There were other assets, but stocks were primarily the principal assets and the first priority was proving ownership, which was tedious at best and they (management) thought it would be impossible, since it hadn't been proven in prior investigations.

Because of my revenue agent experience, it was like taking candy from a baby although the investigation took at least 18 months to complete. The reason for the time was that I did 90 percent of the work (both jobs) since the referring agent honestly did not understand the case. I personally analyzed and reconciled each account similar to bank account analysis. I knew where every dime came from. Of course I had to prove maximum cash on hand since the last investigation before mine was ten years old (but posed no significant problems).

I will say truly that most of the "luggerheads," Group Manager, Assistant Chief, Chief, and Reviewers did not really understand the case, particularly the add-back of non-deductible capital losses and the effect it had on the net worth. But apparently they believed in my technical ability, or I was awfully convincing. The reason for that conclusion, upon preparation for trial, was that I found that I had made a $57,000 error, but had so much money that it was absorbed and to this day no one knows it but me.

At a hearing on motions, lasting about five days, the calculation was reviewed by a Big 8 accounting firm and the only comment was upon disposition of the stock, I should have used "last in, first out." Tax and penalties were in excess of $500,000. The doctor hired a former United States Attorney and after the extensive hearing, the doctor pleaded "guilty" and was sentenced to two years and fined $25,000.

The result was that he quit practicing and tried to conceal his assets after he got out of prison and was again investigated by someone else, but he died shortly thereafter.

The case received considerable publicity because of the doctor's notoriety in the abortion business, resulting in the deaths of several females. (Many investigative agencies were on his trail, but little old me got him.) At the sentencing he (doctor) said that he was never treated better (during all the inquiries) than by me. Strange, huh?

The most interesting case was the one of the public defender. Actually the original investigation was against a Criminal Court Judge of _____, who had very little net worth (though by design), therefore, we thought we could get to the judge through the public defender. Rumor had it that they were "in bed" with one another. This case was a specific item case (of course tying down what was on the return). I had a team of about four agents working with me, as I was the lead agent. We went to city, county and state facilities and federal prisons. Most of the witnesses were African-American and we got testimony of solicitation of assets (insurance policies, cash from items sold—TV, stereo, etc) to be paid to the public defender to prevent a jail sentence. The public defender threatened them by saying if they did not pay, he would see that they got the maximum penalty, which he did if they did not pay. It was told to me that there was a physical sign between the attorney and the judge if money wasn't paid.

After completion of the case, officials were reluctant to prosecute. The attorney hired the son of a Federal Court judge. All involved were prominent attorneys. The case sat in the Justice Department for about two years, and I inquired about the case quite frequently. An enterprising attorney in the Civil Rights Division got wind of the case and conferred with me on the case. He took the case as a civil rights matter, converting the tax information. The public defender was charged with five counts of civil rights violations and found guilty on all five counts, and received five years. How about that."

Assistant Attorney General _____, Civil Rights Division, Department of Justice, Washington, D.C. wrote to the Honorable Donald C. Alexander, Commissioner, Internal Revenue Service, on November 8, 1973 regarding an indictment of the subject for violation of federal civil rights criminal statutes. The letter stated:

Honorable Donald C. Alexander
Commissioner
Internal Revenue Service
1111 Constitution Avenue, NW
Washington, D.C. 20224
Re: Frederick L. Sleet, Group Supervisor
Intelligence Division, Gary, Indiana
Dear M. Alexander:

This Division recently concluded the successful prosecution of _____ pauper attorney _____, for violating federal criminal civil rights statutes in connection with his representations of court certified indigence in Lake County. Our investigation was commenced in 1970 upon notification by the Tax Division of this Department that the Internal Revenue Service investigation of Mr. _____ conducted by your Intelligence Division revealed situations wherein not withstanding Mr. _____'s appointment as a pauper attorney he could condition his representation to his clients on their ability to pay further sums of money. Our subsequent investigation confirmed these allegations and Mr. _____ was indicted.

Pursuant to our formal request, attorneys from this division were permitted to examine the Intelligence Division file on the defendant for a period covering several counts of our indictment and certified copies of the defendant's tax returns were made available. The district judge ruled that our attorneys could cross-examine the defendant and introduce rebuttal testimony with respect to the defendant's failure to include fees, which we alleged he received, in his gross income. We were indeed successful in establishing that the defendant's failure to report these monies on his income tax contributed to the deficiency established by the Service and indicated "guilty knowledge" of the offense charged.

We were able to accomplish this only with the highly commendable and capable assistance rendered us by Mr. Sleet, who prepared the original report as a special agent. As our lawyers were on considerable foreign territory in getting into tax questions, Mr. Sleet's patient and professional assistance was most helpful.

Sincerely,
s/ _____
t/ _____

Fred indicated that he had established himself as an effective special agent, but in hindsight his emotionalism affected his relationships with management. He cited his annual performance rating as a case in point.

In one of his many confrontations with his superiors he advised them that his function was to gather evidence sufficient for a prosecution recommendation, write a report and submit it. He felt that a good report, as to style, was "in the eye of the beholder," and if management wanted to move page three to page nine and move page 50 to page 10, that was their prerogative. He stated, "They could do what they wished, but they could not change my recommendation, and that was the bottom line." Fred felt that this outburst was later used against him when he received his annual performance evaluation. His report writing was rated as average, which prevented him from receiving an overall superior rating. This happened for several years until he decided to play the game. His prosecution record in the district was unsurpassed, and his performance evaluations were as high as attainable. He was still the only African-American special agent in the district, and probably in the Region because Group Supervisor Hilton Owens had been detailed to the Manhattan Joint Strike Force, and Special Agent Curtis Patterson had been killed some years before. As a GS-13 special agent, Fred had no more mountains to climb; no records to break, and nothing more to prove to himself or anyone else. Success did not bring contentment. "It was something one must do," said Fred. "What are you after?" asked his chief. "Your job," responded Fred. It turned out to be a profound statement. Fred's next step was the group manager position in Gary, Indiana.

Chapter Twenty-Four

When the group manager in Gary, Indiana was forced to retire, Fred was advised to apply for the position. As an agent assigned to the Gary post of duty, Fred had served as an assistant group supervisor. After applying, and an interview by a panel, he was telephoned by the chief, who informed him: "You've got the job." He was the first and only African-American in the Indianapolis District to serve as a group manager.

Fred characterized the Gary office as demoralized. There had been allegations relating to his predecessor of having accepted gifts, and consorting with undesirables. When Fred accepted the position he had a frank and lengthy discussion with the chief. He asked the chief to permit him to "Do it my way, and leave me alone. Let me make the promotions, reassignments and no interference in group affairs." The chief agreed. Under the former group manager, the chief had visited the Gary post of duty two or three times per month. During Fred's two and one half years as group manager, the chief did not visit the office. Regardless of the reason for the lack of visits, this gave him the opportunity to turn the group around, or, in the alternative, as Fred put it, "Fall flat on my face." It is a matter of record that he did not fall on his face and the group was a standout in the district, surpassing even Fred's expectations.

Again, it was suggested to Fred that he apply for the vacant assistant chief's position in the Detroit District. "Why me?" Fred asked. "A step up the career ladder," he was told.

His first thought was who would want to voluntarily go to Detroit? But it would be a challenge because he could once again prove he could be successful and not fall on his face, which he thought was expected of him by top management.

This fixation of management's attitude toward him remained throughout his career. He applied for the assistant chief's position and was chosen.

Chapter Twenty-Five

The Detroit Intelligence Division had approximately 110 special agents and 8 to 10 groups. Management consisted of a chief, an assistant chief, eight or ten group supervisors and a staff assistant. Fred stated that he saw his function as being the operational officer. His management philosophy was facilitated by the chief being content to let Fred make the promotions and reassignments and do all the work. According to Fred, "The chief was happy." Fred served as the assistant chief from December 1974 to August 1977.

During those years he described his major accomplishment as follows,

The district director assigned the task of evaluating the Intelligence Division to the assistant district director. In Fred's estimation, it was probably the most scathing report ever prepared. In many circles the Detroit Intelligence Division was considered one of the best in the country. However, the then district director took exception to how the Intelligence Division operated. In his view, the tail wagging the dog. The division had failed to change with the times. Fred was also of the opinion that it would not have mattered what Intelligence Division office had been evaluated, the report would have read the same.

Fred believed that the district director had learned of his management style and apparently saw something that Fred was not conscious of, because Fred was given the task by the district director of preparing a how-to manual whose title became, Detroit District—Intelligence Division—Group Manager's Guide.

Fred stated that he prepared the manuscript at home on his own time, which took the better part of a year to complete. The original document contained a note on the cover page from Fred's secretary, which read:

6-29-77

Mr. Sleet:

Even as I look at this completed guide, I cannot think of all the work it took. Working on it and for you was not 'work,' it was a pleasure!"

Fred indicated that when he left Detroit for the chief's position in San Francisco, his secretary resigned her position in the Intelligence Division.

The introduction to the guide, signed by G.A. Lorenz, Chief, Intelligence Division, read as follows:

> As a group manager in the Intelligence Division you occupy the key management position for the overall administration of our federal criminal tax program. The success of your group operation depends upon your leadership, skill, knowledge, ingenuity and managerial acumen. You are responsible for the results of every phase of your group activity. You conduct operations within the parameter of established policies, procedures, and programs.
>
> There is very little material designed to outline for group managers what is expected of them on their job and how to meet their responsibilities; this void caused the development of this guide. It is not intended for this guide to contain the answers to all questions; rather it is merely a resource to help you do your job better.
>
> If this guide gives you a clearer understanding of only a few of your job tasks, it is worth all the effort expended in putting it together. All Detroit District Intelligence Division managers participated in developing this document; a few selected managers from other IRS divisions provided most valuable review comments.
>
> It is not intended that this guide will ever be completed. It is an ongoing project. Revised and new material will be added as policies and procedures change and when we identify more subject/topics that need comment. You can add your own material as you wish.
>
> Your comments concerning the organization makeup, use, and value of this document are encouraged so that this guide will be more valuable to you on the job.
>
> s/ G. A. Lorenz
>
> t/ G. A. Lorenz

On May 27, 1977 the Director, Intelligence Division, Washington, D. C. wrote to ARC (Intelligence), Central Region, subject: Group Manager's Guide—Detroit District. The memorandum stated:

> We wish to express our appreciation to the Detroit District for allowing us to review their Group Manager's Guide. The Guide contains much valuable information and will be most useful to our task forces responsible for the development of the Functional Management Practices for Intelligence Group Managers course and Handbook for Intelligence Group Managers.
>
> Please extend our thanks to the Detroit District, especially Mr. Fred Sleet, Assistant Chief, Intelligence Division, developer of the Group Manager's Guide for their contribution to the Division.

Sometime in 1977 Fred was advised to apply for the San Francisco District's Intelligence Division chief's position. He did.

Chapter Twenty-six

I recall being in the company of Fred in Washington, D.C. when he received a call that he had been selected as the Chief, Intelligence Division, San Francisco District. I had the impression at the time that Fred was not surprised and certainly did not display any outward excitement. As he pointed out to me recently, he expected to be successful in all of his endeavors; it was something he had to do. "For whom?" I asked. "Certainly not me," he answered. "Possibly your family and acquaintances?" I asked. "Probably, but not for myself," he again reiterated.

The November 18, 1977 issue of a San Francisco newspaper carried the following article:

New Boss for IRS

Frederick Sleet, an Internal Revenue Service employee since 1955, has been named Northern California's IRS intelligence chief here. Sleet replaces retiring Ray Carter as head of the division that investigates IRS criminal fraud cases. He comes here from Detroit, where he has been assistant chief of the intelligence division since 1974. A native of Connersville, Ind., he is a graduate of Anderson College in Anderson, Ind.

The chief's position was double encumbered for about six months, which gave Fred ample time to obtain firsthand knowledge of the Intelligence Division's operation. He was told that there were major problems in the division, which he found to be true as he observed the daily operations.

The division had almost 110 agents in 9 groups. Morale and production was poor. There were 60 over-age cases, which were investigations that were left hanging and no decision had been made as to their criminal potential. The "big happy family" syndrome that prevailed in the district was immediately turned around. The Californians' attitude of "play, play, and play" was also reversed. There had been favoritism where special agents had been promoted to the top (GS-13) without ever having a successful criminal case. In Fred's opinion the assistant chief, and most of the group managers, were his problems. During his three-year tour as the chief, he removed the assistant chief, and all but three of the eight or nine group managers.

The overage cases were reduced from 60 to 5 or 6 in a very short time. It had been one of Fred's priorities to build an inventory of potential criminal cases. He formed an Intelligence Gathering and Retrieval Unit (IGRU) to identify impact cases. The unit tightly controlled and information received was personally reviewed by Fred. Significant criminal cases ensued. In the process, a rapport developed between Fred and his immediate superior, the district director. Fred became his backstop and confidant in district matters, many of which were totally unrelated to intelligence division operations.

Fred indicated that as time passed, he knew that he would not remain in San Francisco as the division chief. He may not have been well-liked, but he was respected. He felt that the Intelligence Division could now be turned over to another chief for all the credit and accolades for the division's success.

The district director approached Fred regarding the Executive Development Program. This program (commonly referred to as the "charm school") prepared managers for the offices of assistant district director and district director. If he attended the Executive Development Program, his goal would then be to become a Regional Commissioner, and in the twilight of his career he felt that it was too late, even if he received a waiver that would permit him to work beyond the mandatory retirement age of 55 for all criminal investigation personnel. He declined the district director's offer of assistance. Shortly thereafter he was advised to apply for the Assistant Regional Commissioner—Criminal Investigation, for the vacancy in the Mid-Atlantic Region, headquartered in Philadelphia. After the interview before a panel screening the applicants, Fred, for the first time, did not have a feeling that he had the position locked up.

His instincts proved correct. He did not get the job. Shortly thereafter, he was given another interview for a similar position in the Southwest Region, headquartered in Dallas, Texas. He had a different feeling about this latter interview. He was appointed to the Assistant Regional Commissioner—Criminal Investigation position for the Southwest Region in August 1980.

Chapter Twenty-Seven

Fred departed from the second interview for Assistant Regional Commissioner—Criminal Investigation position with a distinctly different feeling. In hindsight, he felt that the interview for the Mid-Atlantic Region was actually for the Southwest Region position, where there were many problems. He was named to the position and became the first African-American to attain the second-highest position in the Criminal Investigation Division. I asked him when he was appointed if he still felt five feet six in a tall man's world. His feelings had not changed.

The *Hoosier Revenuer*, an Internal Revenue Service publication for March/April 1981 carried the following article on the front page:

Native Hoosier—new ARC

A native Hoosier, Fred Sleet, has been named assistant regional commissioner, CID, Southwest Region. In 1955 Mr. Sleet began his career with IRS as a revenue agent in Anderson (Indiana). He became a special agent in 1963 when he transferred to Indianapolis. From there he moved to Gary to become a group manager in 1972. Two years later he became the assistant chief, CID, in the Detroit District. He then transferred to the San Francisco District for the position of chief, CID."

The December 13, 1980 issue of a Dallas newspaper carried the following article,

IRS Names Regional Head of Criminal Investigation Activities

Fred Sleet has been named Assistant Regional Commissioner, Criminal Investigation, for the Southwest Region of the Internal Revenue Service headquartered in Dallas.

Sleet is responsible for managing criminal investigation activities for the states of Arkansas, Colorado, Kansas, Louisiana, New Mexico, Oklahoma, Texas and Wyoming.

Sleet began his career with the IRS in 1955 as an Internal Revenue Agent in Anderson, Indiana. In June 1963 he transferred to the Intelligence Division in the Indianapolis Office as a Special Agent. In June 1972 he was selected as a group manager in Gary, Indiana. Two years later, Mr. Sleet was selected as Assistant Chief, Criminal Investigation Division in the Detroit District. In 1977, he became the Chief, Criminal Investigation Division for the San Francisco District.

A native of Connersville, Indiana, Sleet graduated from Anderson College in 1953. He earned his BS degree in accounting and did graduate work at Ball State University in Muncie, Indiana.

Mr. Sleet assumed his duties as ARC—CID in Dallas in September. He has four children: Rick, Cindy, Pamela and Michele. Rick, an Indiana University graduate, is employed by the Urban League; Cindy is employed by General Motors; Pamela, a graduate of Purdue University is employed by Dow Chemical; and Michele is a junior in college.

Congratulations poured in from around the country. Fred accepted them with a grain of salt. In his opinion many of the congratulations had an empty sound, for he assumed that many felt that he was an Equal Employment Opportunity (EEO)choice and won the position because he was African-American. He would prove them wrong again.

He knew that his major stumbling block to success was the Executive Assistant to the Assistant Regional Commissioner, in that he (the executive assistant), felt that he should have received the position that went to Fred. The latter had been advised from several sources that they overheard the executive assistant refer to Fred as "one who would soon be put in his place." Within six months the executive assistant was gone.

There were many problems in the region, such as an inordinately high number of cases rejected by attorneys in the Internal Revenue Service, and declinations by the Department of Justice. There were few cases of impact, and little or no direction by management.

First, Fred made it known that the good old boy network was over. The role of all CID personnel was re-emphasized and districts' intelligence management personnel were required to write programs on group manager involvement and case selection. Fred also deviated from the policy of dealing with the division chiefs and dealt directly with the district directors, a change that did not please the division chiefs. It worked. In his view, his Region was ranked among the best when he retired in January 1983.

When asked who had the most influence on his career, without hesitation, Fred stated, "Roger Plate. He had me formalize in writing things that I had always been doing, but not knowing why."

When asked who during his career had been the most effective Intelligence Division director, he stated, "Johnny O," meaning John J. Olszewski, who came up through the ranks and understood the organization.

Fred offered no explanation as to why he decided to retire, except that he "had enough." At his retirement he asked, "How do spell relief?" "R-E-T-I-R-E-M-E-N-T," was his response.

His retirement date was January 3, 1983. He had served approximately 27 years and indicated that, "I had never had a happy day."

At the start of the interview of Fred for this book, he was still angry over his lengthy career even after being one of the most successful African-Americans in the division. It was his view that with all the accolades, people in high places had expected his failure, as well as the failure of Owens and Patterson, and all other African-American special agents hired prior to him. Fred felt that the system was designed to assure failure for Blacks, all of whom were thrown into that undercover jungle as soon as they joined the agency. One African-American special agent, who came on board prior to anyone in this book, became a victim of the system and was the subject of a continuous investigation by the Internal Security Division, and was forced out of the Service. Another African-American special agent, Curtis Patterson, was killed in 1963, so Fred felt that the African-Americans played the game with a stacked deck.

Our recent four-day, three-night, round-the-clock dialogue was therapeutic for both Fred and this writer. Neither of us had discussed our careers or inner feelings in detail until the marathon conversation at his home and office in Texas. Fred indicated that he was at peace with himself for the first time ever. In short, he was no longer an angry man and more importantly, he felt "as tall as the next guy." He actually acknowledged that he was no longer angry with the military or the Internal Revenue Service, and probably was angry with himself all those years without knowing why.

Anyone visiting Fred's office in Dallas would be in awe viewing the myriad of plaques covering all four walls. They range from 1962, when he successfully completed the Treasury Law Enforcement Officers' Training School in Washington, D.C., to his 1980 Appointment to the Assistant Regional Commissioner plaque signed by the Commissioner of Internal Revenue. Anyone inspecting the plaques would also find that Fred was not only an administrator, but was an expert on the Practical Pistol Course.

There is no doubt that the Regional Commissioner, Fred's immediate superior, had full faith in Fred's administrative abilities in that the latter's files contained eighteen delegation orders signed by the Regional Commissioner appointing Fred to that position during the former's absence from the region.

When Fred was Intelligence division chief in San Francisco, the District Director issued delegation orders on many occasions appointing Fred as Acting District Director during his absence from the district. Fred's personal files are replete with awards, commendations and letters of appreciation from many sources both inside and outside the Service; they are too numerous to mention here, but nonetheless are a matter of record. To Fred, none of the attention he received was a cause for jubilation. According to him, "It was just something to be done."

There are those who still say that Fred was lucky.

Post Retirement

Fred decided to remain in Dallas after retirement. He and a former IRS district counsel formed a partnership specializing in taxes, accounting, and financial planning.

As a Treasury Card holder, Fred concentrated on representing taxpayers before the Internal Revenue Service.

He describes these post-retirement days as the happiest of his life.

When I interviewed him in 1989 he contended that he would be "slowing down" soon. I saw him again in 1990. He had not slowed down, as a matter of fact; his goal is to be worth $10 million before he hangs it up. I reminded him that I have never observed a Brinks truck following the hearse to the cemetery. I do not believe that a change of pace, to stop and smell the roses occasionally, is in his nature. Who am I to give advice to a retiree?. I have difficulty taking advice myself. The main thing is that he is at peace with himself and that is what counts.

PART IV

Chapter Twenty-Eight

The Others

At this writing (1989), there may be ten or more other African-American special agents that served a full twenty years in the Intelligence Division and retired. There are also two other African-American special agents who served in other agencies before transferring to the Intelligence Division, from where they retired. When I refer to special agents I used the term to include all levels in the GS-1811 series (criminal investigators). I personally know of three retirees that served in the Manhattan District and one that served in the Brooklyn District. Also several, including Bill Mannie, served in the Chicago District, and one served as the Executive Assistant to the Assistant Regional Commissioner in the Atlanta Regional Office at the time of his retirement. There were so few in those early years that we are all acquainted. It would be difficult to do because of space constraints in this book, but each of other special agents could tell stories similar to those cited in this book, including the 'horror stories' so common to those African-American pioneers in the division.

Why was the Intelligence Division so slow in appointing blacks to special agent positions in the Service? In 1955, it was obvious to me and Patterson that blacks were sorely needed. There were always long lists of locations where undercover investigations awaited us. One must recognize that in the late 1940s and early 1950s, IRS, nationwide, was just another government agency, not necessarily interested in equal employment opportunities. However, in my view, the Cleveland District was an exception. Many African-American college graduates with accounting degrees could, and did obtain employment in that district.

Pittsburgh—that's another story. It is where the story of African-Americans in IRS Intelligence Division began, with the appointment of George N. Charlton, Jr.

Chapter Twenty-Nine

George N. Charlton, Jr., was born, reared, and educated in Pittsburgh. He received his Bachelor of Business Administration degree from the University of Pittsburgh, with a major in accounting. He joined the then Bureau of Internal Revenue in Pittsburgh in 1948 as a Deputy Collector in the Collection Division. He transferred to the then all-white Intelligence Division in August 1953, and thus became the first African-American special agent in the nation. And that was when his troubles started. Charlton not only served in his Pittsburgh home district, he also worked undercover assignments in other parts of the country, such as Detroit, Boston, Oklahoma City, and Harrisburg, to name a few.

For more than 10 years the Gotham Hotel in Detroit sheltered a number of gambling operations from the police. It was known throughout the country as one of the largest gambling operations in existence. In the early 1960s, Special Agent Charlton was sent to Detroit. Thanks to Charlton, the Gotham Hotel was raided by federal agents. It never recovered and was eventually torn down.

However, agents working undercover always return to their home district after an assignment is completed. After his Detroit success, Charlton returned to Pittsburgh.

One must visualize Pittsburgh in the 1950s and 1960s before the federal government made any serious attempt to fight organized crime. Political and police corruption was rampant, and Charlton was literally thrown into that jungle alone, to investigate the gambling fraternity. The fact that Charlton's superiors would send a lone agent into the streets of Pittsburgh without a partner meant one of two things—his superiors were naïve or just plain stupid, or he was not welcome in the Intelligence Division, and his stay (or survival) would be short-lived. It was sure bet that he would not survive in that jungle. He didn't. He advised his superiors in writing of informants telling him he would be set up, or worse, because he was stepping on too many toes. Even a member of his family had been targeted for police harassment. Whether Charlton's memorandum of his conversations with informants was brought to the attention of the District Director or the Inspection Service by the division chief is not known. Suffice it to say that Charlton remained on the street. ALONE.

As federal raids on Pittsburgh illegal lotteries intensified, due to Charlton's street activity, the lottery operators rebelled against paying locals who were on the pad. The locals would benefit by Charlton's removal from the street. When I recently asked Charlton how he managed to survive on the street for almost 10 years, he stated, "Know-how and luck." Unknown to him that luck would run out in August 1963. He was fired. In an administrative action, he was charged with failure to report an attempted bribe, and failure to properly care for official documents. He appealed all the way to the U.S. Supreme Court to no avail. In a related criminal matter he was indicted, and found not guilty. During this period his professional and personal life were in shambles, from which he never fully recovered. The sequence of events leading up to and including his arrest as set forth in Federal court documents were as follows:

One of plaintiff's duties as an undercover man was to make buys, that is, to place bets on numbers, in such quantities as to sustain probable cause for the issuance of warrants and to produce evidence for trials. At the hearing, evidence was adduced that plaintiff would visit establishments where he had reason to believe a bet could be placed and he would attempt to do so. If he succeeded in placing bets and if he received a slip evidencing the same, plaintiff would make some annotation on the back of the slip. As soon as reasonably possible thereafter, plaintiff would prepare a handwritten memorandum describing in detail what had happened in connection with the bet. This memorandum together with the bet slip would be retained on his person, often in a briefcase in the trunk of his automobile. On his next visit to the office, which might be as long as a week later, he would turn in all the slips and the memoranda he had prepared.

In order to perform their job more effectively, agents in Charlton's position had to blend with the environment in terms of dress and hours kept and it was often necessary to drink on the job. They frequently had to make decisions on their own in the field and it was essential to maintain secrecy in contacting the office. Plaintiff's working habits were therefore informal and unconventional.

On August 13, 1963, while in an establishment known as the B & M Tavern, Charlton was introduced to one Bill Ferraro who offered to assist him in getting into seven or eight local numbers establishments, if he would forget about the B & M Tavern. Ferraro then made an appointment to see Charlton the following day.

On August 13, after having met with Ferraro. Charlton called Mr. Green, his Group Supervisor, and stated, "I have a surprise for you," and pursuant to the usual practice in such cases, no details were stated.

On August 14, Mr. Davis, Chief, Intelligence Division, Internal Revenue Service, was informed by one Officer James of the Pittsburgh Police Department that Charlton was trying to shake Ferraro down and that the payoff would take place shortly at the B & M Tavern. Davis insisted that Internal Revenue Service agents accompany the local police officers to the Tavern.

Later that same day, Charlton met Ferraro in front of the B & M Tavern. At this point, Charlton had the numbers slips and memoranda relating to the B & M Tavern in his pocket. The slips and memoranda as to other numbers operations were in his briefcase in the trunk of his car.

After Charlton refused to enter the Tavern, he and Ferraro conversed briefly in Charlton's car. Charlton asked for the names of the numbers establishments. Ferraro said he didn't have the information but that there "might be something else in it for you. Maybe $1,000." Charlton said, "forget it," and claims that he did not consider this to be a bribe offer.

Charlton and Ferraro then left the car to view an accident that had occurred nearby and Charlton lost sight of Ferraro. When Charlton returned to his car, he saw Ferraro standing near the car talking to Officer James. At about the same time, Internal Revenue Agents appeared at the scene.

Charlton was taken into custody and his car was searched. Five twenty-dollar bills were found between the back rest and the seat. Charlton denied all knowledge of the money and maintained that he never intended to accept any money or to turn over slips and memoranda to Ferraro.

On August 23, 1963, Charlton signed a one-page statement wherein he admitted to having received a bribe offer on August 13, 1963, and admitted that he was going to give Ferraro the numbers slips and memoranda. Plaintiff claimed that the statement was extracted by his superior and that he was threatened with dismissal if he refused to talk. The Hearing Officer decided to consider the statement and held that "a statement such as the one in question cannot operate to convict Charlton by foreclosing all further inquiry. At most, it can only be considered as one of the factors in the case, and must be read in light of Charlton's explanations, provided, of course, they are logically satisfactory."

The plaintiff (Charlton) contends that a review of the entire record in this case leaves little doubt that the government's dismissal action was arbitrary and capricious.

Administrative action may be regarded as arbitrary and capricious only where it is not supportable on any rational basis. The Hearing Officer, having analyzed the record and all other available evidence, in sustaining Charge I, i.e., failure to report an attempted bribery, concluded that under the circumstances Ferraro's statement to Charlton was an obvious offer of a bribe; that the circumstances of this case point to some sort of bribe offer being made to Charlton on August 13, 1963; that Charlton's call to Green on August 13 cannot be construed as a report of the incident; that it would have been readily possible for Charlton to report the bribe offer and that Charlton's failure to report the bribe offer had not been shown to have been due to criminal intent.

The Hearing Officer did not sustain Charge II, i.e., failure to properly care for official documents on the grounds that Charlton had a perfect right to the possession of the slips and memoranda found on him at the time of his meeting with Ferraro.

The Regional Commissioner, Internal Revenue Service, having reviewed the entire record, sustained both charges against Charlton. The record is not clear as to the purpose of using the services of a Hearing Officer if Service officials can ignore the former's findings. The Regional Commissioner sustained both Charge I and Charge II, on the following grounds:

I find the charges upon which removal was based, both Charge I and Charge II, to be supported by the evidence. The facts relating to Charge I establish that M. Charlton received a bribe offer, which under the circumstances he must have recognized as such and that he failed to report this offer within a reasonable period of time. Charge II is sustained on the basis of evidence that he retained official documents, namely, numbers slips and memoranda concerning them, which he had prepared as part of his official duties, with the intention of delivering them to a person not authorized to receive them; further, that he performed acts pursuant to this intention sufficient to warrant the conclusion of the District Director that he had failed to properly care for official documents.

The Civil Service Commission's Philadelphia Regional Office, upon review of the entire record in sustaining Charlton's dismissal stated,

In essence, the appellant contends that the agency has not shown cause for his removal other than the charged technical violations of agency regulations.

We believe that the significance of the appellant's actions, and in particular his failure to report the attempted bribe, is apparent from the circumstances in the case . . . By the appellant failing to report the bribe offer, made by 'Bill,' to the servicing Inspection office (or to anyone in authority at the agency), the agency was embarrassed (to say the least) and left without any evidence of before-the-fact knowledge of the scheduled meeting of "Bill" and Mr. Charlton on the afternoon of August 14, 1963, and the bribe overtures made by 'Bill' on the 13th, when the Pittsburgh Police Department apprised the agency of the meeting that was to be held between 'Bill' and Mr. Charlton on August 14. Had Mr. Charlton complied with Subsection 1941.73 of the Rules of Conduct and reported the bribe offer, not only his integrity but that of the agency would have been protected.

Because of Mr. Charlton's long and wide experience in the field, the agency concludes that his failure to report the bribery attempt was deliberate.

The record reveals that Mr. Charlton exercised much initiative in performing his duties and that he was given wide latitude by the agency to act independently. However, he was still bound by the requirement to recognize and report bribe overtures so that trained personnel could evaluate the facts. The indications are that Mr. Charlton elected to bypass the servicing Inspection office in order to negotiate a deal with "Bill" to obtain the information that would assist him in making seven or eight cases.

The appellant's actions in the subject case have given the agency cause to question whether his excellent past record for "making cases" did not result from similar agreements.

> The Civil Service Commission concluded:
> Our ultimate finding is that the agency action was taken for such causes as will promote the efficiency of the service within the meaning of the language in the Civil Service Regulations.

The Civil Service Commission's Board of Appeals and Review, having reviewed the entire appellant report including all information developed during the processing of appeals, in sustaining Charlton's dismissal, found that all charges, specifications and related evidence had been fully and properly considered.

The Court, having made a careful and thorough review of the entire administrative record before it, is satisfied that there is a rational basis for Charlton's dismissal and that the agency's action is therefore not arbitrary and capricious nor an abuse of discretion. The Court is satisfied that the evidence in the record supports both charges and establishes that Charlton failed to report an attempted bribery and that he improperly retained certain numbers slips on his person at a time when other such slips were in the trunk of his car.

The Court finds that the evidence supports the conclusion reached by the Regional Commissioner, Internal Revenue Service, and the Civil Service Commission that Charlton retained the slips on his person with an intent to deliver them to an unauthorized person for an improper purpose.

It is not improper under the circumstances to disregard the conclusion of the Hearing Officer, who did not sustain the second Charge, and to rigorously interpret the standards of conduct to which agents in Charlton's position must be held. This did not prejudge Charlton's character or personality nor the facts of the case.

Charlton, a college graduate, who had been a special agent for about ten years and had been engaged in undercover work for about five years, was an experienced individual who knew of his obligation to the Internal Revenue Service with respect to the conduct with which he was charged and failed to maintain the high standards of conduct formulated by the Service for its employees. The lack of criminal intent found by the Hearing Officer as to Charge I is irrelevant under the circumstances.

The review of the administrative record also discloses that the agency's action is supported by substantial evidence . . .

Order of Court, and now, to wit, this 28th day of May, 1971, it is hereby ordered and directed that the defendant's motion for Summary Judgment be and hereby is granted, and judgment is hereby entered in favor of the defendants, United States of America and John W. Macy, Jr., J. Judwig Andolsek and Robert E. Hampton, Members of the United States Civil Service Commission, and against the plaintiff, George N. Charlton, Jr.

s/ John L. Miller
United States District Judge

In the United States Court of Appeals, for the Third Circuit, Case No. 16-670, the U.S. District Court for the Western District of Pennsylvania, the decision of the district court is affirmed.

Of particular interest in the Appeals Court decision was one paragraph that said it all:

"At the same time, the Court does not review the matter de novo nor does it substitute its own judgment or wisdom for that of the agency exercising its judgment to remove an employee." (citations omitted).

In short, the appeals process applies as to whether the agency followed procedures and not whether sound judgment was used in the process.

Charlton recently confided in me that much to his regret, under threat of being fired, he signed a statement that he had been offered a bribe. He further contended that when his vehicle was searched, the agents did not attempt to hide the fact that they knew exactly where to look for the "hidden" money. Even more interesting, an attempt was made by the IRS Inspector to have Charlton remove the currency from where it was hidden, on the pretext of having him count it. Charlton advised the Inspection Service agent that the removal of the currency by him would result in the currency having his fingerprints and he would not be that stupid, because the bills had been "planted" and did not contain his prints.

Now-retired government sources suggested that there was much conjecture in federal law enforcement circles as to whether a racketeer, the police officer, or the IRS Inspector planted the currency in Charlton's automobile. It was purely an academic question, inasmuch as the money was not relevant to Charlton's subsequent dismissal.

This case is cited to illustrate how the first African-American special agent hired in 1953 was treated, and the climate that existed in the Intelligence Division at the time. The matter is closed, and the truth is a moot point. Most of the retirees who worked undercover for a great many years would look back at Charlton's situation and say, "But for the grace of God, go I."

How could any government official, regardless of his lack of knowledge about the "ghetto jungle," construe the comment, "There may be something in it for you, maybe $1,000," as a bribe offer. The agent's response, "forget it," lends credence to the belief that it was just "street talk" that takes place constantly.

Each time Special Agent Charlton hits the streets, his life was on the line. In a criminal case, he was found not guilty of any improprieties. In the administrative dismissal, his denials fell on deaf ears, but that is understandable. Pittsburgh in the 1950s and 1960s was no better for African-Americans than Mississippi, Georgia, or Alabama, at that time.

Having personally spent thousands of days and nights in the streets and ghettos of rural and urban America, my view of Charlton's situation is probably biased. Be that as it may, irreparable and unjustified damage was done to Mr. Charlton's reputation, career, and livelihood. At the time Charlton was having his troubles with the Service, no less than three other special agents in the Pittsburgh District had even more serious problems. They were brought in from the field until things settled down, and then returned to duty. Not surprisingly, they were white.

Chapter Thirty

For Charlton, employment in the federal establishment came to an end. But he was resilient and bounced back with positions such as Executive Director, Public Parking Authority of Pittsburgh; Executive Director, Pittsburgh Model Cities Program; and he rose to the rank of Lt. Colonel in the Army Reserve, and is a graduate of the U.S. Army Command and General Staff College. One must wonder how far Charlton would have advanced in the Intelligence Division, or elsewhere in government for that matter, if he had not been born African-American in Pittsburgh, or even more important, had not become the first African-American special agent in that city in the 1950s. What is so ironic is that Charlton's dismissal was "all so legal," just as the hangings of Blacks were in Mississippi during that era. Funny thing, when I recently interviewed Charlton, he did not appear bitter, at least not as bitter as I would have been. He simply stated, "Hilton, get my badge and pocket commission back for me. My legacy to my children will not be complete without them." I left his home without comment, but he knew that I would tell his side of the story because it is so much a part of the IRS African-American history.

EPILOGUE

Chapter Thirty-One

"Remembering the past while focusing on the future"

The above was the motto of the Association for the Improvement of Minorities in the Internal Revenue Service. The Association held its 20th Anniversary Annual Business Meeting and Training Seminar at Philadelphia from August 8 through August 13, 1989. I was among the 750 persons that attended and was unprepared for what I witnessed; African-American professionals equal to professionals anywhere. That was not the case when I retired. What was most significant to me, as probably one of the oldest persons in attendance, was the number of African-American women in attendance and the impressive management positions they now hold in the Service. I believe that in my lifetime I will witness women outnumbering and outranking their male counterparts in management positions. Not because they are the so-called weaker sex receiving special treatment, but because they now have the drive, momentum, credentials, background, and the opportunity to achieve their goals. You guys take notice.

Newly appointed IRS Commissioner Fred T. Goldberg made a touching speech at the Convention. During the 30-plus years I worked in IRS, I witnessed a number of Commissioners in action. All of them were not friendly, or even neutral toward blacks. This gentleman, and I sincerely mean "gentleman," who carries a heavy personal burden, is obviously well aware of the plight of African-Americans and other minorities in the Service. After his speech he hastily departed to catch the train back to Washington, D.C., but returned to the podium and emotionally apologized for using the term "you people." To me it was an innocent remark, and was used in the narrow sense of addressing the persons attending the convention. It had other connotations for many of those present. Such a gesture on his part took character and courage and gave the audience an insight into the man. Only time will tell, but I believe that all minorities will receive a 'fair shake' from him. Pursuant to an earlier request I made to the former Commissioner, I received some very interesting statistical data regarding the Service, and in particular the African-Americans in CID.

The Internal Revenue Service had over 100,000 employees that processed 194 million tax returns in 1988. Gross revenue receipts totaled $935.1 billion and 83 million refunds were made, totaling $94.5 billion.

IRS examined 1.03 million returns, which resulted in $19.2 billion recommended additional tax and penalties.

CID, whose mission is to encourage and achieve the highest possible degree of voluntary compliance, reported1988 statistics as follows:

*Summary of Criminal Investigation Division Activity

Activity	Number
Investigations initiated	4800
Investigations completed	5000
Prosecutions recommended	3044
Indictments and Information	2769
Convictions	2441
Sentencing	2619
Number receiving prison sentence	1590

The above statistics, obtained from the Commissioner's1988 Annual Report, relate to investigations of tax shelters, tax protesters, narcotics, money, finance, and regular cases.

The EEO program was also addressed in the annual report and stated in part:

"IRS made significant advances in its Equal Employment Opportunity (EEO) Program. The IRS sponsored several conferences for women and minorities A Black Executive Conference addressed issues concerning elevating Black managers to the upper levels of the IRS as well as strengthening the numbers of Black candidates in the lower levels of the IRS"

It was interesting to note that 1988 was the beginning of the Service-wide EEO Hall of Fame Award.

The following is a schedule of criminal investigators(special agents) on the rolls as of December 31, 1988:

Grades (GS)	Total	5	7	9	11	12	13
Total	2723	56	222	225	313	791	1114
Percent	100	2.1	8.2	8.3	11.5	29.0.	40.9
Female	531	20	77	77	115	192	50
Percent	19.5	7	2.8	2.8	4.2	7.1	1.8
Black `	197	8	17	21	41	80	30
Percent	7.23	.3	.6	.8	1.5	2.9	1.1
Female	67	1	8	8	17	2	4
Percent	2.46.		3.	3	.6	1.1	.1

The following is a schedule of management (supervisory)criminal investigators on the rolls as of March 31, 1989:

Grades	Total	13	14	15
Total	493	51	385	57
Percent	100	10.3	78.1	11.6
Female	34	7	25	2
Percent	6.9	1.4	5.1	.4
Black	26	4	20	2
Percent	5.27.	8	4.1	.4
Female	6	1	4	1
Percent	1.22	.2	.8	.2

I was unable to obtain information from the National Office regarding the identity of the 26 African-American supervisor/managers; however, I learned from other sources their identities and locations. They represented about 5percent of the 506 managers in the division at the time.

During the previously mentioned AIM-IRS Convention I was in the company of many of the managers for three days and evenings and they freely voiced their respective views, even with the knowledge that I was in the process of preparing a historical document regarding African-Americans in CID.

There was only one official Functional Breakout period at the convention for CID, but the enthusiasm and interest generated by the discussions resulted in two additional sessions, one of which I generated.

I posed what appeared a simple question that suggested a simple yes or no answer. I informed the group that now retired Assistant Regional Commissioner—Criminal Investigation, Frederick L. Sleet, and Group Manager William E. Mannie were of the opinion that any African-American in CID could advance as far as he or she desired in the division. It required eleven minutes (I counted) to get the group quiet enough to have individual persons voice their opinions to the group. I might point out that I did not expect yes or no answers, but certainly did not expect such violent verbal reactions.

Robert L. Thomas, Chief of the Cincinnati District at the time, responded most eloquently on the subject, but he too, refused to give an unqualified yes or no answer. He reluctantly gave a qualified and restrictive "Yes" that opportunities were unlimited. He pointed out that the best and most effective tool any agent has is a comprehensive file reflecting his or her track record. "Never assume that someone, somewhere, will do this for you." I am thoroughly familiar with Mr. Thomas' track record. He was not aware of the fact that I had watched his career very closely over the years. Suffice it to say that he "paid some heavy dues," and never fell into that "you owe me because I'm African-American syndrome," which is so prevalent these days among African-Americans. It may not be grammatically correct but "Nobody owes you nothing," so keep that in mind each workday of your career. There is an old saying that goes: "If you look back in the sand and fail to see your footprints, somebody is carrying you." When I began gathering material for this book many years ago I reminded myself not to knowingly embarrass anyone, but I deviated from that and will probably embarrass former Cincinnati CID chief, Bob Thomas, who epitomizes those no-nonsense, godlike chiefs of bygone days that we young and eager special agents of yesteryear tried so much to emulate. His stoic, expression-less and sincere demeanor is most deceiving. That may account for his many successes. But instinctively, he could revert to a reassuring smile, reach down and offer a helping hand not only to his subordinates, but anyone in need. That is the type of leader whose briefcase I would not be embarrassed to carry. Recently, at the AIM-IRS convention, Bob placed a hand on my shoulder and stated, "Can I ask you for a favor?" I answered in the affirmative without asking the nature of the favor, because Bob is not the type of person to ask anyone for favors. He appeared to be quite emotional, which is so unlike him. I said, "Name it," to which he said, "Would you give me your autograph?" It dawned on me that he was quite serious. In the interim between the request and my feeble "yes" response, so many thoughts passed through my muddled brain, such as why would one of the highest-ranking officials in the division want my autograph. I may have been a pioneer but certainly not worthy of throwing my autograph around like some time-honored hero. Nevertheless I scribbled a short note to Bob, which I embarrassingly signed, and in turn, asked him for a return favor, which was, "Don't retire as soon as you are eligible. African-Americans will need you more than ever in the coming years." This dialogue between Bob and me took place during one of those informal breakout sessions and did not go unnoticed by others present, who apparently convinced Bob that he is a natural leader and the higher the position he achieves in the Service, the more assistance he can be to the individuals and the Service in general.

Others voiced their opinions regarding opportunities, or lack thereof, for African-Americans, and were cautiously optimistic as to their respective futures. If I could offer the up-and-coming managers any advice it would be not to worry so much about their own career(s), but help those less fortunate, and in the process they will be surprised how much such assistance would help to broaden their perspective. Such help will not go unnoticed.

We (Owens, Mannie, and Sleet) are in general agreement that opportunities are limitless for the best qualified, dedicated and highly motivated African-Americans in the Criminal Investigation Division. As college recruiters in the past, we experienced considerable difficulty in recruiting minorities, as is evident from the above statistics.

During the earlier years of the Equal Employment Opportunity Program, the salary structure in government was not conducive to recruiting top African-American college graduates, because they generally received more lucrative offers from the private sector. The IRS salary structure for professionals has continually improved over the years. *Special Agents in the GS-5, 7, and 9 grades were promoted up to GS-11. Beyond that point promotions were competitive; based on availability and grade structures in the particular district where the special agent is assigned. However, current statistics show that more than 40 percent (40%) of field agents are in the highest field grade attainable.

It should be noted that the journeyman grade for special agents was GS-11, but is now GS-12.

Sleet, Mannie and I still consider the federal government, and particularly the IRS, a fascinating career worth pursuing.

APPENDIX

Appendix A-1

There are many taxpayers that undoubtedly have been successful in cheating on their income taxes, thus far. There are also many persons that probably could be temporarily successful at Russian roulette. If you insist on "trying your luck," there are a few basic rules for would-be tax cheats, i.e., deal only in cash, do not confide in your spouse, boyfriend or girl-friend; bury your ill-gotten gains in a tin can in your backyard, mattress, or attic; do not make any enemies in the family, workplace or community; do not attempt to keep up with the Joneses; be wary of cocktail parties; and avoid Swiss and Cayman Island bank accounts. Human nature being what it is, who can follow these few basic rules that are necessary to be a successful tax evader? There will always be persons trying to beat the odds. One of the reasons more persons are not prosecuted for attempted tax evasion is due to the Service's limited resources. The following is an illustration of a hypothetical case in which a fictional couple tried their luck. In IRS the special agents' role-playing by students in the classroom settings made the scenarios even more realistic. The would-be tax evaders are:

John and Mary Bigbucks
123 Upper Crust Drive
Mountain Top, Michigan 48111

Information was received from an anonymous source that John and Mary Bigbucks must be cheating on their income taxes, because they purchase two new luxury vehicles almost every year; live in a mansion on the hill overlooking the city; take frequent trips to Las Vegas and Monte Carlo; and John "spends money like there is no tomorrow." The anonymous source further stated that John Bigbucks bragged of "paying just enough taxes to get by," at a cocktail party where he had too much to drink.

The Internal Revenue Service receives literally tens of thousands of such allegations each year. Suffice it to say that the Service, through a sophisticated system of processing and evaluation, decided that the Bigbucks matter should be further pursued. The IRS Criminal Investigation Division entered the picture. An inspection of several years of Bigbucks' tax returns indicated that preliminary inquiries were warranted. Also, the tax returns of their wholly owned corporation did not reflect any transactions that could account for the alleged free-spending Bigbucks. Real estate, motor vehicle and other records available to the IRS indicated that Mr. and Mrs. Bigbucks were living well beyond their visible means. The case was assigned to Special Agent U.R. Caught, who determined that the taxpayers should be advised of the criminal investigation, and asked to come into the office for an interview. In the interim, the special agent requested an Internal Revenue Agent from the Examination Division to cooperate in a joint investigation.

The special agent's function was to obtain the evidence necessary to prove guilt beyond a reasonable doubt in the criminal proceedings, and the internal revenue agent was responsible for the civil (technical) aspects of the case.

Special Agent U.R. Caught and Internal Revenue Agent I.C. All, visited Mr. and Mrs. Bigbucks, and introduced themselves as a special agent and an internal revenue agent respectively, and furnished their pocket commissions (identification) for the taxpayers inspection. This was a crucial point in that case, or in any criminal investigation, and if not properly done, the taxpayers could, and generally will claim that they were deceived as to the seriousness of the matter. After the introductions, Special Agent Caught read the following from a document that all special agents carry in their credentials. He stated, "As a special agent, one of my functions is to investigate the possibility of criminal violations of the Internal Revenue laws, and related offenses."

"In connection with my investigations of your tax liability, I would like to ask you some questions. However, first I advise you that under the 5th Amendment to the Constitution of the U. S. I cannot compel you to answer any questions or to submit any information if such answers or information might tend to incriminate you in any way. I also advise you that anything which you say and any documents which you submit may be used against you in any criminal proceedings which may be undertaken. I advise you further that you may, if you wish, seek the assistance of any attorney before responding. Do you understand these rights?"

If both taxpayers respond in the affirmative the special agent may again explain their rights, and ask both taxpayers if they wish to retain an attorney before answering any questions or furnishing any documents. Mr. and Mrs. Bigbucks both stated that they understood their rights. Mr. Bigbucks indicated that they were totally unfamiliar with taxes; had an accountant handle their financial affairs; had nothing to hide; but would feel more comfortable if their attorney was present during the interview. Bigbucks agreed to telephone the special agent in a few days and arrange a mutually agreeable time and date for the interview. The agents departed, returned to the office, and prepared a detailed memorandum of the meeting, which both signed. The following day the taxpayers' attorney telephoned Special Agent Caught and the conversations went something like this,

Attorney:	"Hi, U.R., this is Reele Mean. How are things going since I retired?":
Special Agent:	"Fine, I'm keeping busy as ever. You really did a good job training me."
Attorney:	"Say, what's this about you investigating Mr. and Mrs. Bigbucks?"
Special Agent:	"Reele, you know I can't talk to you unless you have power of attorney.
Attorney:	"Right, I'll get the formed signed today. How about meeting me at our old lunchtime hangout and talk about it. I'll bring the power with me."
Special Agent:	"No can do. Check with your clients and let me know when they can come in for an interview and get back to me as soon as you can. Oh yes, send me a copy of that power of attorney. It was nice talking to you again. Take care."
Attorney:	"Right, U.R. See you soon. Regards to the wife."

Special Agent Caught made a note on his appointment calendar to telephone the attorney if the power of attorney was not received within a week. About 10 days later the special agent telephoned the attorney's office and was advised that Attorney Mean was out and would returned his call later in the day. No call was forthcoming. One week later the special agent, accompanied by the revenue agent, visited the business establishment of Mr. Bigbucks, unannounced, and met briefly with the taxpayer. The latter advised that he and his wife had executed a power of attorney about two weeks earlier and was waiting for Attorney Mean to schedule the interview. Mr. Bigbucks telephoned his attorney and the agents left the room for Mr. Bigbucks and his attorney to confer in private. Shortly thereafter, the agents were summoned back to Mr. Bigbucks' office and the latter gave the telephone to the special agent.

Mean:	"I've talked to the accountant and return preparer. You're just fishing. I can't let the taxpayer see you."
Caught:	"If they have nothing to hide, why not let me interview them?"
Mean:	"I tell my clients never to talk to a special agent, because no matter how polite he is, he's trying to put you in jail, so don't help him."
Caught:	"Tell your client that we don't put people in jail. We just gather all the facts and let the chips fall where they may."
Mean:	"Well, you just gather what you think are the facts, and when you finish, let me know. One other thing, if you compel my clients to appear they will not produce any records or answer any questions, so why waste your time and mine?"

Further, the agents were requested by the attorney not to contact the taxpayers in the future and should deal through him only. Special Agent Caught advised the attorney that until such time as he received the power of attorney he would deal directly with the taxpayers. By the time the agents reached their office, the power of attorney had been delivered by special courier.

Mr. and Mrs. Bigbucks were majority stockholders and officers of Widgets Inc., a relatively small company that had been in the Bigbucks' family for several generations. The agents opened an investigation of the corporation as well, and the corporate officers (John and Mary Bigbucks) were notified by registered mail.

During the following week the special agent served a summons on the company comptroller for his appearance and for the production of all the corporate books and records for the period under investigation. A summons was also served on the tax return preparer for his appearance and for the production of his work papers relating to the corporation.

The taxpayers and their corporation were separate entities, and as such, the 5th Amendment privilege with respect to the corporation could not be invoked by the taxpayers. The company comptroller and the return preparer could be compelled to appear with the items listed on the summons, and failure to appear could result in civil and/or criminal penalties.

The comptroller appeared as scheduled with the corporate books and records and appeared to cooperate fully. The agents retained the records for sufficient time to photocopy them in detail, including correspondence files, bank statements, canceled checks, and deposit tickets.

The revenue agent's in-depth examination of the records did not disclose any irregularities. The records verified the items of income and expenses on the corporate return. The records also verified the salaries reported on the Wage and Tax Statements, Form W-2, issued to each of the taxpayers. The dividend income reported by the taxpayers agreed with the corporate records.

The tax return preparer appeared for interview as scheduled and also appeared to cooperate fully during the questioning. His work papers failed to reveal any information other than that reported on the individual and the corporate returns. His work papers were also photocopied in their entirety.

After the interview of the comptroller and the tax return preparer, the agents concluded that any unreported income to the corporation and/or the individuals did not flow through the corporation. The comptroller and the return preparer were cognizant of that fact from the outset. They apparently so indicated to the taxpayers' attorney, who appeared at the special agent's office with Bigbucks' savings passbooks and certificates of deposit. The special agent, in the company of another special agent, photocopied the documents and returned them to the attorney. In departing, the attorney stated, "If I were still your boss, you'd have to close this case and let the revenue agent disallow a few dollars for travel and entertainment. You've got nothing else." The special agent responded, "In that case, why not let me interview the taxpayers." "I see no need for that," stated the attorney, who then departed.

The special agent served summonses on banks with which the taxpayers and their corporation conducted business, requesting all documents for the period under investigation.

He then went about obtaining documents and testimony from the person who sold them their present home, which they had occupied for about five years. He also obtained testimony and documents from travel agents, jewelers, department stores, and automobile dealers. While their expenditures seemed inordinately high for their reported income, it was not sufficiently high to discount any claim by them that they lived within their means.

The banks produced their savings accounts, certificates of deposit and also their checking account monthly statements, and deposit tickets. The savings accounts and certificates of deposit agreed with the documents furnished by their attorney.

The checking account monthly statements, and deposit tickets, were turned over to the Internal Revenue Agent for his scrutiny. He was already in the process of examining all corporate checks and deposit tickets.

The revenue agent and special agent met and reviewed their actions to date to plan a course of action. Both were of the opinion that they undoubtedly missed something during their examination of the books and records of the corporation or the accountant's work papers. Revenue Agent All advised Special Agent Caught that he had corresponded with the customers of the corporation for verification of purchases by them and he begun to receive responses. According to the revenue agent, the amount reported as purchases by the customers agreed with the corporate sales record. A common scheme of corporate officers "raking it off the top" appeared remote.

Internal Revenue Agent All excitedly telephoned the special agent and advised that he had found that a photocopy of a dividend check payable to Mary L. Carson that had been drawn on Fidelity Trust, Eugene, Oregon. The endorsements were unusual in that they contained Mrs. Mary Bigbucks' signature, and also the signature of one Mary L. Carson, and a series of numbers thereon. What was Mary Bigbucks connection with a bank in Oregon? More importantly, who was Mary L. Carson?

Special Agent Caught forwarded a photocopy of the dividend check to the Criminal Investigation office in Portland, Oregon, and requested that their office contact the bank teller regarding the endorsements on the check. The special agent in the Eugene, Oregon office, telephoned Special Agent Caught and stated, "If you're looking for what I think you are, you hit the jackpot. The bank teller is well-acquainted with Mary L. Carson. She married John Bigbucks some years ago and moved away, but visits her widowed mother every two or three months. She also maintains a small office in her mother's home."

The special agent suggested to Special Agent Caught that a summons be served on the bank and also on the telephone company, which their office in Eugene, Oregon would serve.

Special Agent Caught agreed and advised that he and Revenue Agent All would visit when records became available.

About three weeks later the agents visited Portland and met with the Chief, Criminal Investigation Division. He introduced them to Special Agent Allan Gregory of their Eugene office, with whom Special Agent Caught had briefly spoken on the telephone. The chief requested that they keep him apprised of the situation in the event there were any tax violations in his district.

The agents inspected the telephone company records and learned that in addition to a personal telephone at the address, there was also a business telephone. The personal telephone was in the name of Mrs. Anna Mary Carson, and had very few long-distance calls. The business telephone was in the name of Northwest Widget Products, an affiliate of Widgets, Inc. with numerous long distance calls, but bunched at two or three-month intervals. Special Agent Caught and Revenue Agent All readily recognized the residence and business telephone numbers of Bigbucks and their corporation.

The bank's signature card for Northwest Widget Products authorized Mary L. Carson, treasurer, a/k/a Mary Bigbucks, to make withdrawals, transfers, or otherwise dispose of all checks payable to Northwest Widget Products. The signature card listed John Bigbucks as alternate. The bank records also listed a post office box address as well as a street address. The deposits to the account averaged $50,000 to $60,000 over a three-month period and withdrawals every three months averaged the same amount.

The post office advised that the application for the box was submitted by Mary L. Carson, for Northwest Widget Products, and the box rent was paid promptly. The mail was picked up promptly by her mother, Mrs. Anna Mary Carson.

With the documents and information obtained and its impact on the case, Special Agent Caught telephoned his group manager, briefed him on the situation, and suggested that he and Revenue Agent All remain in the area and obtain statements (affidavits) from those persons involved. He further suggested that Mrs. Anna Carson be interviewed as soon as possible. His supervisor agreed.

Special Agent Caught and Internal Revenue Agent All interviewed Mrs. Carson in her home the following day. She absented herself for a few moments and returned, advising them that she "put on the teapot and would enjoy their company with tea and biscuits." They diplomatically declined, and she seemed to understand. She was very cooperative and related the history of the family; her daughter's marriage and business career; and the generosity of John, her son-in-law. She went on to state that her husband left her only a small annuity, and that coupled with her social security, she could just about make ends meet. John and Mary supplied her with spending money, paid her monthly mortgage, and whatever else she required, including a new car. She stated that the car came in handy because she hated walking to the post office to pick up the mail several times per week. She stated that the mail was held for her daughter on the desk in the basement office, and volunteered to show the agents the accumulated mail in the basement. The agents declined. Before departing Special Agent Caught asked Mrs. Carson several questions:

Caught:	"Did your husband leave your daughter any money or property in his will?"
Mrs. Carson:	"Oh no, there was nothing to leave her. What little there was, he left to me."
Caught:	"Did you ever see any large sums of money hidden around the house?"
Mrs. Carson:	"There was never more than a few dollars around the house."
Caught:	"Could there have been money around the house that you did not know about?"
Mrs. Carson:	"Impossible. When my husband was alive, there was always something we wanted

	but could not afford. If he had any money hidden I would have known."
Caught:	"Then neither you nor your husband gave your daughter any large sums of money?"
Mrs. Carson:	"No. It was the other way around. She and her husband gave us money from time to time to help us."

The agents departed, advising Mrs. Carson that she might be contacted in the future for a formal statement.

When they returned to the IRS office, Special Agent Caught was advised to contact his group manager back in his home district. His supervisor advised that Attorney Mean had telephoned several times to confer with the special agent, and insisted on getting in touch. The supervisor declined to furnish the special agent's whereabouts and a shouting match ensued between the two former co-workers. The supervisor prevailed, but assured the attorney that Special Agent Caught would contact him immediately upon his return.

Special Agents Caught and Gregory, and Revenue Agent All, estimated that there was several months of work awaiting them in the Eugene, Oregon area. Caught and All returned to their home district to confer with their superiors.

Shortly after arriving in the office Caught telephoned the taxpayers' attorney, who requested an immediate conference. Caught advised him that early afternoon was fine and telephoned Revenue Agent All of the scheduled conference.

A docile and nervous attorney appeared for the conference and furnished the agents a new power-of-attorney, representing Mrs. Mary Bigbucks only. He further stated that he was not at liberty at this time, but hopefully in the near future he would permit Mrs. Bigbucks to repeat the same story to the agents that she had related to him. The attorney went on to state that Mrs. Bigbucks was visiting her mother in Oregon, and was also picking up some records. Upon her return in a few days they would schedule a date and time for the interview. Special Agent Caught asked if the records related to the corporation, and the attorney responded, "Indirectly, yes."

Attorney Mean telephoned the special agent a week later and they agreed to meet the following morning.

The conference consisted of the special agent, revenue agent, attorney, and a very nervous Mrs. Mary Bigbucks. Special Agent Caught asked Mrs. Bigbucks if Attorney Mean had advised her of her constitutional rights and she answered, "Yes, he did."

"Do you understand your rights?" asked Special Agent Caught.

"Yes, he explained my rights to me."

"Fine," said Special Agent Caught, "but I must read you your rights in accordance with IRS procedures." Special Agent Caught read the following from a document:

As a special agent, one of my functions is to investigate the possibility of criminal violations of the Internal Revenue laws, and related offenses.

"In connection with my investigation of your tax liability I would like to ask you some questions. However, first I advise you that under the 5th Amendment to the Constitution of the United States I cannot compel you to answer any questions or to submit any information if such answers or information might tend to incriminate you in any way. I also advise you that anything which you say and any documents which you submit may be used against you in any criminal proceedings which may be undertaken. I advise you further that you may, if you wish, seek the assistance of any attorney before answering. Do you understand these rights?"

Mrs. Bigbucks responded: Yes, I understand."

At this juncture Attorney Mean suggested that before the "routine" questioning Mrs. Bigbucks be permitted to repeat the story she had related to him a few days earlier. Special Agent Caught asked the taxpayer and her attorney if they objected to the interview be recorded. Mr. Mean stated that they did not object if they could have a transcript of the interview. Special Agent Caught informed them that they would have an opportunity to review the statement and if Mrs. Bigbucks signed it, they would be furnished a copy.

Mr. Mean stated that he would advise Mrs. Bigbucks to sign the statement if they would be furnished a copy.

Special Agent Caught asked Mrs. Bigbucks to stand and raise her right hand. She did. He asked, "Mrs. Mary Bigbucks, do you swear that the statement you are about to make will be the truth, the whole truth, and nothing but the truth, so help you God?" She stated, "I do," and was advised to be seated. She then related a story of a stormy marriage; a business career that was a charade; a domineering and violent husband; and his scheme to accumulate great wealth without anyone knowing. She related how she pleaded, cajoled and cried, in her futile attempts to get him to give up the "jet set" style of living and revert to those happy days during the early years of their marriage. He would have no part of it, and told her that if she did anything to "rock the boat," he would, "cut off all money to your mother, divorce you, and take off for Switzerland or Mexico" with their accumulated wealth. While talking, Mrs. Bigbucks was fumbling through the material she brought and produced her husband's passport. She stated that any planned sudden departure to a foreign country would be forestalled, at least temporarily, when he could not locate his passport.

Mrs. Bigbucks frequently digressed, but after approximately three hours she finally finished. Special Agent Caught suggested they break for refreshments. Mrs. Bigbucks and her attorney departed, while Caught and All remained in the conference room, almost in shock.

The taxpayer and her attorney returned and Special Agent Caught advised Mrs. Bigbucks that she was still bound by the oath she took before the conference commenced. She stated that she understood and finished her startling story. The special agent advised Mrs. Bigbucks that he and Revenue Agent All would like the opportunity to examine the records she brought and would she object to leaving them for a few days? They would furnish her a detailed receipt of the documents retained. She advised that she would prefer the records remain with the Internal Revenue because her husband would stop at nothing to get them. Internal Revenue All asked Mrs. Bigbucks if she had any idea of how much money had been received and not included in their reported income. Mrs. Bigbucks stated that the records in the carton beside her would accurately reflect the exact amount, but she would guess that it was approximately $150,000 to $200,000 per year for the past six or seven years. She was asked by the special agent if she knew that these monies should have been reported on their income tax returns. She stated, "Yes, and John and I argued about it every year at tax time."

She was asked if John knew how much money they omitted from their tax returns each year. She stated, "He knew better than I did, because he kept track of every dollar, and told me to put the money in bearer bonds."

"How much do have in bearer bonds?" asked Caught.

"About $1.6 million would be my guess. There is a list of the bonds and the dates purchased in that carton beside you," responded Mrs. Bigbucks.

Special Agent Caught asked Mrs. Bigbucks if she would permit the agents to inspect the bonds. Attorney Mean intervened, and stated that the bonds could be inspected, listed, and photocopied, at his office the following day. Thereafter, they would remain in a safe place until disposition was made of any criminal case. Attorney Mean advised that although the husband/wife privilege existed, Mrs. Bigbucks was willing to cooperate as much as possible, including what disposition should be made from the proceeds of the bonds. Attorney Mean advised that Mrs. Bigbucks could be reached only through him, because she would be in hiding for the foreseeable future.

The agents spent the better part of the following day photocopying the bonds, which totaled 1.8 million.

A conference was held the following day which was attended by the Chief, Group Supervisor, and Special Agent, Criminal Investigation Division, as well as the Internal Revenue Agent, his immediate supervisor, of the Examination Division, and a member of the District Counsel's office. The district director had been invited, but had a prior commitment. He was later briefed and agreed with the decision to treat this as a regular case, on a need-to-know basis.

Special Agent Caught's top priority was to have Mrs. Bigbucks review and sign the statement, for fear of a change of heart on her part. Within a week Mrs. Bigbucks and her attorney reviewed the statement and he advised her to sign it, which she did, after initialing each page as requested by the special agent. Caught and All signed the statement as witnesses.

John Bigbucks signed a new power of attorney several months later, and his new attorney advised that Mr. Bigbucks would make a statement "at the appropriate time." Special Agent Caught made several attempts, without success, to interview Mr. Bigbucks during the remaining 10 months it required to complete the investigation.

Insofar as the special agent was concerned, the most damaging testimony to any possible claim of innocence by Mr. Bigbucks came from Mr. Mannheim, treasurer, Western Export Corporation. The latter advised that when they became a customer of Widgets Inc., Mr. and Mrs. Bigbucks met with him and Mr. Bigbucks advised that they were forming Northwest Widget Products, a warehousing affiliate. Bigbucks requested that all payments for merchandise shipped be paid directly to the affiliate. Mr. Mannheim was shown a photograph of Mrs. Bigbucks and stated that the person introduced to him at the meeting was not the person in the photograph.

At the conclusion of the lengthy investigation, the Chief, Criminal Investigation Division, offered each taxpayer an opportunity to discuss the case and furnish any additional information or explanations before he made a final decision as to the disposition of the case.

Mrs. Bigbucks appeared with Attorney Mean for the conference and advised the chief that she had cooperated fully in the investigation. She further stated that the agents were perfect gentlemen and she had no complaints in that regard. She stated that there was no doubt in her mind as to her husband's guilt, but extenuating circumstances had dictated her course of action, i.e., the threats of her husband regarding her mother, and possible danger to her own life. She thought that her husband might do her mother bodily harm in attempting to learn the whereabouts of the bearer bonds, if she, Mrs. Bigbucks, divulged their scheme. The chief advised Mrs. Bigbucks that he appreciated her honesty, but the extenuating circumstances would not enter into his decision to concur or not concur in the special agent's recommendation for prosecution. He further advised Mrs. Bigbucks that the matters she discussed would be for the court's consideration. Attorney Mean advised the chief that the bearer bonds were still kept in a safe place and the bonds would be discussed with the Service upon disposition of the criminal case. They again thanked the agents for their courtesy and the discreet manner in which they handled the investigation. That terminated the conference. Special Agent Caught prepared a detailed memorandum of the conference, which was signed by the chief and the agents.

John Bigbucks did not respond to the letter offering him a final conference. The chief forwarded the case to the next level of review for further consideration.

There were five levels of review, each of which concurred in the Special Agent's recommendation for prosecution. The final decision rested with the U.S. Attorney, who also concurred.

Special Agent Caught heard rumors of plea bargaining, as will happen with most cases, but that was not his concern.

The case was put on the Court's calendar, and separate trials for husband and wife were granted.

The case cited above is a composite of several actual cases to illustrate the complexity of issues encountered by agents on a daily basis. Such cases are used as training tools for special agents attending the Service's school.

However, the schools such as the aforementioned Special Agents' Basic School carry the training a step further, in that they set up a realistic mock trial, including judge, jury, prosecutor, defense attorney, and witnesses. The instructors advised that over the years the juries returned surprising verdicts. That was because certain testimony was inadmissible, trained evidence was "thrown out," husband/wife privilege raised many issues, and defense attorneys attempted to create a reasonable doubt of guilt. We were constantly warned by our instructors that proving a criminal tax evasion case was as difficult as proving murder in the first degree. In tax cases there is no smoking gun. Events that happened several years previously must be reconstructed in an atmosphere of hostility and reluctance on the part of witnesses testify truthfully and openly. Most often the witnesses are friends, business associates, and family members. To prove guilt beyond a reasonable doubt, the admissible evidence must show that, (1) a taxpayer had income that he/she did not report, (2) that they were aware of the income, (3) and that the failure to report the income was willful. Proving items (1) and (2) is painstaking, but not difficult. However, proving item (3), willful intent, is the most difficult part of any criminal investigation, in that an evil motive or bad purpose must be shown. The case of John and Mary Bigbucks would be no exception. During our earlier years in the Intelligence Division, John and Mary Bigbucks, if convicted of attempted evasion of income taxes, could each receive sentences of five years and $10,000 fine for each year convicted. Sometimes the five-year sentences ran concurrently. Since 1982, the fine was increased to $100,000 for each account.

Attempted Evasion vs. Failure to File

The following is a simple comparison of what many "tax experts" consider tax law that cannot be adequately explained to the public.

Consider Smith and Jones, self-employed professionals, living side by side in an affluent suburb of Atlanta. They are married and each have two school-age children. Smith decided that he would not file income tax returns because the tax rates were too high and the government in Washington, D.C. was spending our tax dollars unwisely. John, on the other hand, was not afraid to file. He and wife submitted joint tax returns each year, but reported about 50 percent of their income. He too, felt that the tax rates were too high and the politicians squandered our tax dollars. Both wives admonished their respective husbands about "flirting with disaster."

Over a 10-year span, Smith paid no income taxes, while Jones paid approximately $100,000 in taxes, or about one-half of what should have been paid. Let us assume that Smith and Jones' earnings were about the same and they were in the same tax bracket.

If the Smiths, who paid no taxes, were convicted of willful failure to file tax returns, each could receive a maximum of one year in prison and a fine for each year convicted. On the other hand, if the Jones' were convicted for the attempted evasion of income tax by reporting only one-half of their income, they each could receive a maximum of five years in prison and a fine.

This may be an oversimplified illustration, but "half a loaf is worse than none." The above is another scenario of topics that were heatedly debated at the Service schools, but only in an academic sense. Congress passed the law and only Congress can rectify it, if it needs rectifying.

It should be noted that willful failure to file returns are considered acts of omission, while attempted evasion is considered an act of commission. Thus, certain acts, too numerous to cite here, performed by persons failing to file tax returns, have elevated their misdemeanor case to the felony category.

Appendix A-2

Law Enforcement Officer Training
United States Treasury Department
Washington

In 1927 the Treasury Department began to operate a law enforcement training school covering the basic principles of enforcement law and criminal investigation. The first classes conducted by the school were for supervisory officers. The course was two weeks long. Instruction was mostly by lecture, and instructors traveled to field sites to conduct the training.

In 1951 the school converted from a three-week course conducted by traveling instructors to a four-week course conducted in Washington, D.C. In 1953 the school was reorganized to provide for more student participation and practice, and in 1955 the course lengthened to six weeks.

Today, the classes in the basic Treasury Law Enforcement Officer Training School cover many more subjects because of advances in technology and more sophistication in enforcement law and criminal investigation work. Basic courses still include films, skits, role-playing, practice problems, laboratory work, mock crimes and trials, evaluation critiques, and written exams, with about half of the total training time devoted to active student participation and practice.

During the period that we attended the basic Treasury Law Enforcement Officer Training School of six weeks for all Treasury Agents, other types of schools and institutes were held each year providing training of a basic, supplemental, advanced, of specialized nature in enforcement law and criminal investigation.

At the present time the average age of the students in the basic school is between 25 and 30. Average length of service in Treasury law enforcement work prior to attending the school is less than two years. About 60 percent of the students have had four years or more of college or professional education, while about 30 percent have had some college but less than four years.

Since 1927 more than 560 schools have been held, graduating a total of more than 14,000 students.

The school's facilities are made available to the seven law enforcement activities of the Treasury Department.

A Treasury Agent must meet Office of Personnel Management standards as to education, experience, and physical requirements. He or she must have training in police science, police administration, or law—or experience in criminal investigative work—and meet high standards of physical ability. Inquiries and applications for employment as a Treasury Agent are made directly to the particular Treasury agency concerned or to the U.S. Office of personnel Management.

Attending the Treasury schools today are a limited number of enforcement personnel and officials from other agencies and governments—federal, state, municipal, and foreign—that cooperate closely with the Treasury in law enforcement responsibilities.

NOTE: Some of the above information is undoubtedly outdated, but informative as to the period when the subjects of this book were still part of the IRS.

When Curtis Patterson returned from school in early1957, he had been given the impression that he was the first African-American special agent to attend that particular school. Also, school officials notified the Cleveland District Director that Patterson had ranked number one in his class. During my research for this book, I learned that Patterson was not the first African-American to attend the school.

That distinction of being first goes to Special Agent George N. Charlton, Jr. He attended in late 1956. Special Agent Bruce Murray and I followed Patterson, attending in the summer of 1957. Even today I look back on those days as one of the highlights of my career. First, I made a lasting friend in Bruce. We often reminisce about those wonderful days of more than thirty years ago when the District of Columbia seemed like a small slumbering town with streetcars, small restaurants, happy hours galore, and no fear of walking the streets at night. All that is gone now.

Those six weeks of training included surveillance techniques, firearms qualification (indoor and outdoor combat shooting), fingerprinting, self-defense, interviewing and interrogating, Federal Court procedures, rules of evidence, laws relating to other federal crimes, and a most realistic mock trial of an alleged violator of the internal revenue laws. I did not realize it at the time but that mock trial would forever be the basis for my conduct on the witness stand as the government's principal witness in the real world where defense attorneys used every trick in the book to discredit the agents' testimony. During the time I later testified in open court, and there were many, my mind invariably went back to the grilling we received during that mock trial in school.

When I attended the school, the students consisted of agents from all agencies in the Department of the Treasury (Secret Service, Intelligence Division, Alcohol, Tobacco and Firearms, IRS Internal Security, Narcotics Division) and law enforcement officers from foreign countries. A high ranking law enforcement officer from the Philippines and I became rather close during those six weeks and corresponded for some years after. As will become apparent throughout this book, my career took an unusual turn that isolated me from family, friends, co-workers, and acquaintances for many years. My Philippine friend and I lost contact.

I suppose that those weeks in Washington in 1957 are still so vivid in my memory because I looked at the city through the eyes of a tourist. Our formal training required photographing specific targets around the city, developing and printing the film in the school's lab. By coincidence, my wife visited the weekend scheduled for the photography project, and she also fell in love with Washington. Our photo albums will attest to the beauty and tranquility of that city in the early 1950s.

Insofar as the curriculum was concerned, neither Bruce Murray nor I had any difficulty. We parted with the usual promises of keeping in touch, as most people do in similar circumstances. We kept our promise and are still the best of friends and get together, but not as much as we promise each other each time we write or call.

In discussing Washington, D.C. with other special agents, it seems that their memories and nostalgia of that brief six-weeks were best summed up by one of the subjects of this book, Bill Mannie, when he stated, "*I loved it, I loved it.*"

About The Author

Hilton returned to his native Cleveland from the Virgin Islands in the fall of 1993. Hilton, and his wife of 49 years, are again enjoying retirement. They have three children and two grandchildren. Both his daughter Beatrice, whom he refers to only as "Pumpkin," and her husband Kenny, are longtime telephone company employees. His oldest son, Hilton Jr., is a professional draftsman, and the "baby," Jerome, is a nineteen plus year veteran (Supervisory Criminal Investigator) with the Internal Revenue Service. All of the children, including their son-in-law, are college graduates.

Hilton is still intrigued with white collar crime and is presently accumulating research to do a possible follow-up on his doctoral dissertation, which was titled, "An Analytical Review and Plan for Combating White-Collar Crime."

If there are any idle hours left, his hobbies of chess, photography, jazz music, and personal computers will certainly fill the void, and finally, he still holds a current Treasury Card, authorizing him to represent taxpayers before the Internal Revenue Service, and he may occasionally take on the agency's bureaucrats.

Researching the material for this book and writing the original manuscript, even before the input from Fred Sleet and Bill Mannie, was a labor of love. In retrospect, he tried to remain objective, but Fred Sleet and Bill Mannie are friends and objectivity may have suffered somewhat.

He found it easier to write about them than himself. Putting together his thoughts in a logical manner was a very emotional undertaking. Seeing his thoughts, actions, and feeling on paper was even more heart wrenching. It seems that Fred Sleet and Bill Mannie experienced even more difficulty because their respective twenty-plus year careers on paper is so abbreviated. Several requests from the author for additional information from each of them met with unusual silence.

Bill Mannie had given this much thought over the years and included in his section of the book is a self-portrait. Hilton's interview of Fred Sleet suggested a self-portrait, but he could find no such revelation in his own history or career. His best friends, Danny Bonomi and his brother Albert, suggested at the outset that he find a ghostwriter for his section of the book, but Hilton chose otherwise. If there are any two people, in addition to his wife Beatrice, who know what makes Hilton tick, it is Danny and Albert. He reluctantly, with much misgivings, to include their combined unabridged views as to "how he did, what he did" and survived. Whether Hilton agrees with his brother, Albert, or his friend, Danny, is academic, because success and/or failure is "in the eye of the beholder."

Albert And Danny

When the original concept of writing a book was first mentioned to me by Hilton Owens, I immediately gave it the go sign. It was something that I had known he should do, but I had no idea as to how he should do it. Since he is the only person who could possibly write it, my introduction is very easy. But to portray an accurate, and yet objective narrative about the author will not be so easy. In addition to being a very good friend who followed his career, Hilton is also my brother.

It takes a certain amount of talent, knowledge, education, and sheer determination for a person to succeed in his profession. All of the above qualities are found in Hilton. But even more is needed to be highly successful and be able to look back on a brilliant career, second to none. What makes this person so astounding in his profession is that there were no role models preceding him along the lonely paths he had to blaze. Hilton has the rare talent to be honest, fair, and above all, never to think that he is better than anyone he has ever met, only more fortunate.

Hilton also has the ability to blend in with his immediate surroundings, regardless of where the location would be or the people involved.

His sense of fair play goes back to our childhood days. In addition to having to protect me from my big sister Margaret, (she is two years older), he would also challenge the older and bigger boys in the neighborhood because he knew his older brother, Fred, should have a sense of fair play also, and come to his aid.

Hilton continued to *think* fair play even after his brother left him to fight alone.

The night he concluded his most successful assignment, I was at his residence. He unlocked the door, came in, and locked the door. Then he took a deep breath, looked at the floor without seeing it, and said in a low voice, "Well, it's all over." The expression on his face was one that not many can see in a lifetime. It revealed the culmination of all of his early dreams, desires, hopes, and frustrations. It was a summation of the years of education, training, prior experience, learning, and knowledge of people. It was a look, burned into my mind, that I cannot forget. It also showed some happiness and a touch of sadness, a sense of pride for a job that was "well done." With a sigh, the look was gone and he became Hilton, the brother again.

Our parents had dreams of success and achievement. In their era, dreams were only dreams. But in our adult lives, dreams come true. In this instance it did. I have a poem that I saved from my early years. I think it would be appropriate at this time to dedicate it to both my father and brother . . .

GREATNESS

A man is as great as the dreams he dreams
As great as the love he bears,
As great as the values he redeems,
And the happiness he shares.

A man is as great as the thoughts he thinks,
As the worth he has attained
As the fountains at which his spirit drinks,
And the insight he has gained.

A man is as great as the truth he speaks,
As great as the help he gives,
As great as the destiny he seeks,
As great as the life he lives.

—Author Unknown

Dan Bonomi, a colleague of Hilton for about thirty years, provides a moving testament of the other half of the professional life of my brother, Hilton.

Albert Owens

One would find it very difficult to attempt an in-depth dissertation of the man, Hilton Owens. First of all, if you really know him, it is immediately apparent that you are dealing with a multifaceted, multitalented subject. Secondly, the knowledgeable person knows that it may be impossible to deal with this subject exclusively and not find oneself tripping over the activities of his wife Beatrice and his brother, Albert Owens.

I met Hilton Owens a little less than thirty years ago The first major project and joint effort involving Hilton and I turned out to be the National Office Undercover Group. Even though there were five or six experienced undercover agents at these conferences, it was very obvious that most of the attendees frequently deferred to Hilton's ideas and suggestions. During these meetings it also became apparent to me that he was the only other person in the room who had engaged in infiltration undercover as well as fringe types and understood some of the things that I proposed to the task force. Infiltration experience and fringe type experience have nothing in common; yet many people involved in undercover work simply lump the two as though they are the same.

While this information regarding his experience intrigued me, the personal relationship still took time because, as with me, there appeared to be imbedded in him one of the many cardinal rules of undercover work, "Talk little and listen a lot."

Our next meeting took place a few months later at which time we were selected as two principal instructors for the undercover training program. During this time, he and I established residency at the Catholic University Holiday Inn in Washington, D.C. Each day we (instructors and administrators) met to review, refine and practice our lecture and lesson plans. In the evenings he and I returned to the Inn at which time we ate dinner and discussed the training material and our personal and professional experiences in order to present a true and effective schooling session. It was then that I was strongly impressed with the first two of his many hobbies. First, the ever-present, regardless of where we went, complex camera, and second, the portable tape playing stereo and his extensive collection of tapes.

Herein lies one of the first sides of this complex man. Ingeniously, he decided to carry a camera while on undercover assignments. The advantages of a camera on assignment were tenfold. But you had to carry a complex camera or people would catch on.

As would be expected, during our discussions, I was amazed at his knowledge of and expertise with the camera and photography.

With regard to the stereo systems and tapes, I had considered myself fairly good with taping, dubbing, copying and reproducing, until I met Hilton. His ability and craftsmanship led me to conclude that this man didn't simply take up a hobby, he took it apart, reformed it and made it another facet of his life. If he was interested in something, he took full control. As strongly impressed as I may have been, over the years I began to realize that those two activities should have been the harbingers and a cameo view of 'Hilt.'

Owens had no pathfinders or role models in government when I met him. He did have a 'load' at the time that I was able to discern. Among other things to deal with, he lost a longtime partner and fellow agent in a tragic situation. Nevertheless, he had become the pathfinder and role model for many agents that have followed.

Hilton shared all that he had with the others on a daily basis. As a result of his tours across the country to interview prospective undercover agents for the National Group; while assigned as the Intelligence Division representative to the New York Strike Force; and as a member of the Operations Branch in Washington, he had more contacts with other Special Agents than any agent. He gave of his knowledge, experience, expertise and even, in the case of a know-it-all young agent, his snappy tongue.

I recall the time when one of the young agents at the school began explaining to the benign looking Hilton what a complex game chess was and it would take too long and too much to explain to Hilton in detail. Owens abruptly left and within minutes returned, told the agent to sit down; opened the chess board set and soundly beat the young man at one of the fastest chess games I had ever see. The next day he sought out the man and did the same thing over again. Subsequently, the young man was heard to remark, "It's hard to get whipped by one of those guys that doesn't yell or say much, that instructor is pretty intelligent." On the other hand I recall a young agent at one of the training schools with tremendous personal problems, almost to the extent of being out of control. Hilton personally took the man by the hand every night, weekends and during any free time the man had. He was father-confessor, big brother, protector and leader. The compassion and sensitivity was running from 'Hilt' as though it were a tangible thing.

He was indefatigable, full of energy, and love for the job. He was also sometimes righteous. Well, being his own pathfinder with no role models, one would truly have to agree, he had it all together and could afford to be righteous because he was also always sincere.

When I first got to know him, as I said, multifaceted yes, but a façade? truly, an enigma? Yes. What kept him level, controlled, and enthusiastic? Was there really a well-rounded man?

Sometime later, I felt very privileged. I was invited into his home. By this time, I had met Beatrice (Bea) and his 'pumpkin' (the beautiful daughter). I ate many meals and slept many nights at their home at times while the children were there. Therein lies another part of the whole man. One saw a family filled with love, thoughtfulness and consideration; and the glue that keeps it all together, makes it all possible and likely for Hilton, the perfect help-meet personified, "Bea." You simply cannot take Hilton alone, you cannot leave Bea out. If the truth be told, I received some of the best advice regarding my personal life from Bea.

While associating with Hilton one finds you cannot be close to him and not Albert Owens. Knowing Albert explains more of Hilton. They are very close and over the years he relied on Albert for many things. Albert is also a self-made man, an expert on computers, and stereo intricacies, intelligent and personable. Hilton has made his way through life as he would have planned. I think that he made life. There are times when he gives the impression that he is a driven man, i.e., thirst for further education, projects, businesses, knowledge and travel. But then, this is not an epitaph, let's wait and see.

Hilton Owens is a remarkable man; a proud man; he has very good reason to be.

Dan Bonomi

Notes From The Editors

(Republishing Original Book)

Hilton Owens
1924-2007

Hilton Owens, Sr., was born on January 21, 1924 in Cleveland, Ohio, graduated from Central High School in 1942, and served 4 years in the U.S. Army. Hilton started with the Veterans Administration in 1947 and went on to earn a Bachelor of Business Administration degree from Western Reserve University (1953) in Cleveland, Ohio and his masters (1977) and doctorate (1978) degrees from California Western University in Santa Ana, California. Owens transferred to the Internal Revenue Service in 1951 where he retired as a Special Agent, Intelligence Division, in 1975 ending thirty-one years of federal service. His last position was with the Department of Justice "Manhattan Joint Strike Force" against Organized Crime.

A "pioneer" is described as "one who goes before, preparing the way for others" which perfectly describes Hilton. In the law enforcement world where he accomplished these feats required more than the norm. It was done in a spectacular manner that had little or no margin of error to survive. Some are described in *Three of The First*. With his knowledge and expertise, Hilton was in demand after retirement, here and abroad.

After an amazing number of successes, unparalleled in African-American history, Hilton decided to again enjoy his retirement years. With his beloved wife of sixty years (who preceded him in death), they traveled thousands of memorial miles with their daughter and son-in-law, 2 sons, 3 grandchildren, and his brother and sister-in-law. While the city was preparing for another day, sunset came to Hilton Owens, Sr., the morning of July 12, 2007.